Also by Jimmy Carter

# CHRISTMAS IN PLAINS

*Memories*

Jimmy Carter

Illustrated by Amy Carter

Simon & Schuster

New York   London   Toronto   Sydney   Singapore

SIMON & SCHUSTER
Rockefeller Center
1230 Avenue of the Americas
New York, NY 10020

SIMON & SCHUSTER and colophon are registered trademarks
of Simon & Schuster, Inc.

For information about special discounts for bulk purchases,
please contact Simon & Schuster Special Sales:
1-800-456-6798 or business@simonandschuster.com

Book design by Ellen R. Sasahara

Manufactured in the United States of America

1   3   5   7   9   10   8   6   4   2

Library of Congress Cataloging-in-Publication Data is available.

ISBN 0-7432-2491-4
0-7432-6065-1

To my family,
and to the people of Plains

# Contents

★

# CHRISTMAS
# IN PLAINS

# Introduction

★

This book is a description of some of the Christ-mases that have been important to my family and me, from my childhood on a farm through eleven years in the U.S. Navy, then later to the Governor's Mansion, the White House, and back—always when we were able to go home to Plains, or just longing to be there.

In all that time, Christmas has been a season of mixed interests and meanings, but the very founda-tion, of course, is its religious significance. No mat-ter what other personal desires or crises we have faced, I've never forgotten that this is the time to celebrate the birth of the Baby Jesus, and the impact of this event on the history of the world.

Although this underlying premise has never changed since my earliest memories, it is remarkable how much my perspectives of Christmas have varied down through the years. I have to admit that, as a child, my anticipation of Santa Claus and gifts was dominant, regardless of any religious reminders. There were times when I was almost totally obsessed with the presents I might receive, and had only secondary thoughts about giving, even to my parents or sisters. Later, there was the added attraction of a few days of vacation—both from school and from work.

The first time I gave much thought to giving was when I was trying to gain an advantage in competing for the favors of a popular teenaged girl in high school. I wanted my present to be the best one she would receive.

All during those early years, I took for granted that I would be enclosed within the protective cocoon of my immediate family. After I left home for college and the Naval Academy, Christmas holidays brought an alleviation of homesickness, and a chance to be back in Plains with my family and old friends.

When I finally fell in love, my sweetheart and I established a new and unshakable desire for Christmas: to be together and to please each other. I was in the navy during my first seven years of marriage, and had to accommodate whatever circumstances were imposed on my family by superior authority. Having three little boys changed the focus of Christmas completely, and we tried to resurrect the pleasant memories of our own childhood and give our children the joy of place and belonging that we had known. Our earlier desire to receive gifts was now gone completely, as we focused on bringing surprise and delight to our own children.

When we were able to return home to Plains, we had to learn how to balance the demands of our two widowed mothers, both strong-willed and demanding as matriarchal leaders, dividing the hours of Christmas Day so as to please both of our families. Fortunately, all of us had our lives centered in Plains. It was not until our sons married and had their own families that the benefits of our annual family reunion were shattered by the competitive demands of our fellow grandparents.

Both as a naval officer and in public office, as the

First Family in Georgia and then the nation, we often had duties that took precedence over our strong desire to be with family, preferably in Plains. This home community has been central to what has been most often—but certainly not always—a joyous time of year. Finally (at least for now), with our parents and all my siblings gone, we have been challenged to devise means of holding our expanding family together, and, once again, Christmas gives us the answer.

Christmas, family, and Plains—the three are inextricable.

# 1

# Christmas as a Child

★

To understand what Christmases were like when I was a child, one has to know a little about where I lived and, of course, the times. I grew up on a farm in Southwest Georgia during the days of the Great Depression. In *An Hour Before Daylight*, I described my life in the rural community of Archery, about three miles west of town. Our family moved from Plains to the farm in 1928, when I was four years old. U.S. Highway 280, then a narrow dirt road, was fifty feet in front of our house, a modest structure whose plans had been provided by Sears, Roebuck and Company. Paralleling the road was the Seaboard Airline Railway, heavily traveled in those days by both passenger and freight trains.

But now everything has changed. There is usually only one train a day, and most of the people have moved away. With the coming of modern transportation and the legal end of racial segregation, people have gone their separate ways, and the intimacy between black and white folks has disappeared. But Christmas is still as important as ever, both in its religious meaning and as a time for friends and relatives to get together.

\*

In those earlier days, all my close neighbors were black families. Johnny and Milton Raven, Edmund Hollis, and A. D. Davis were the intimate friends with whom I played, fought, fished, hunted, slept, ate, and worked in the cotton and peanut fields that were owned by my father. The other boys lived down the road a half a mile, but A.D. stayed on our farm with his uncle and aunt, and he was an inseparable companion. In a way, the adults had given us to each other.

When I was five years old, Daddy arranged for me to begin selling peanuts during the summer months, as soon as the crop began to mature. I would go into one of the fields, pull up a small wagonload of vines out of the ground, haul them to our yard, pick off the nuts, wash them carefully, soak them overnight in salty water, boil them early the next morning, and put a half-pound in each of about twenty paper bags. Then I would walk down the railroad track to town and sell the boiled peanuts on the street for a total of about a dollar, usually finishing this task by noon. But even with this daily routine and my time in school, I always felt that I was in an alien environment when I was in Plains, away from my black friends and with the "town folks," the white children who were my age, and in the unfamiliar places where we sometimes played together.

In my earliest memories of Christmas, beginning about 1930 and including my childhood and formative years, I was closely encapsulated with just a few others: my parents, my older sister, Gloria, and our baby sister, Ruth. (My brother, Billy, came along much later.) My father was a landowner and also had a small commissary store adjacent to our house, so our relatively prosperous family life was similar to those of our relatives and friends who lived in Plains, and the quality of the gifts we exchanged was also equal to theirs. Compared to those of our black neighbors, with whom I spent most of my time, Christmas days for us white folks were isolated islands of affluence.

The Great Depression was a time of almost incredible poverty, not only in Southwest Georgia but all over the country. Although my father was a landowner, cash money was scarce for us and for everyone else. Land seemed to have the only permanent economic value, and hard work was the key to survival. The celebration of Christmas during these times was quite different from what we know today: much more frugal, but with a degree of personal intimacy that brings back warm recollections.

# 2

# My Family

★

My father, Earl Carter, was a successful farmer and businessman who—like everyone else in the community and, indeed, the nation—abided by the U.S. Supreme Court ruling that "separate but equal" treatment of the races was the law of the land. So far as I knew, this premise was never questioned in those days by either white liberals or black activists. Daddy was known as someone who cared for his land, made good crops, was honest, and treated people fairly. He was an outstanding baseball player, a good diver, hunter, and fisherman, and the best tennis player in the community. My father was my idol, and my highest goal in life was to please him and to enhance my value as a worker on the farm.

When I was a baby he began calling me Hot Shot, and for the rest of his life I was "Hot." I always knew I was in trouble when he shifted to the more formal "Jimmy."

My mother, Lillian, was a registered nurse, who served almost as a doctor in our remote Archery community. Both by temperament and as a member of the medical profession, Mama ignored the racial distinctions that were the bedrock of our Southern rural society. On most days, neither of our parents was at home during daylight hours, and at work or play we children were immersed in the culture of our black neighbors.

Mama and Daddy were avid baseball fans, and usually took a summer vacation to see games in a different major-league city each year. When they were away on these weeklong excursions or just for one or two nights, I stayed with Rachel and Jack Clark, whose house was the one nearest ours. It was a tiny shack, with a small bedroom, a larger space with a fireplace, and a shed in back for a kitchen. Rachel fixed me a pallet stuffed with corn shucks on the floor, and would let me move it so I could sleep close to the fire on cold nights. I was perfectly at home there. I knew, of course, that Jack was almost coal-black and Rachel was light tan, but in those boyhood days I never gave a thought to differences between them and me because of color.

Jack Clark was the only person on the place who was employed every day of the year. He was in charge of the barn and livestock, and he joined with Daddy in teaching me how to perform my duties on the farm. His wife, Rachel, took me to pick blackberries and plums, helped me in the cotton and peanut fields, and taught me moral values, respect for God's natural world, and how to catch fish in the local creeks. The Clarks were surrogate parents for me.

\*

Other than my mother and father, black people mostly shaped my life. Although my father was a prominent landowner, the person who gave me a vision of fame and fortune was Bishop William Decker Johnson, the richest and most prominent citizen of our community. He was successful in every way, being responsible for churches in five Midwestern states and the founder and proprietor of a small college and an insurance company in Archery. It was news for the whole area when the bishop came home, riding regally in his chauffeured Cadillac or Packard.

Bishop Johnson was a friend of my father's, and on special occasions he would invite our family to hear his powerful sermons in St. Mark's church, just across the railroad tracks from the Johnson Home and Industrial College. My friends told me about their great Christmas celebrations at the church and school.

**3**

# Christmas Events

★

There were a lot of cycles that affected our lives. The seasons of the year controlled priorities on our farm. The cold winter months were devoted to working in the woodlands, repairing fences and buildings, slaughtering hogs, curing meat, harrowing land for shallow burying of last year's crops, and terracing fields to control erosion.

Springtime was for planting, beginning with corn, then cotton, and finally peanuts. After that came a frantic struggle with grass and weeds, in which hoes and plows were employed almost constantly until the growing crops were so near maturity that the movement of mules and people up and down the rows did more damage than good. The only fieldwork during the resulting lay-by time was the reaping of winter wheat. Next came the major harvest season, when corn, cotton, and peanuts were started on their way to the barn or market. Daddy always did his best to ensure that all the slack intervals were filled with caring for beef cattle, milk, chickens, sheep, sweet potatoes, sugarcane, watermelons, tomatoes, and garden crops.

One very important division of the year for me was between wearing shoes and going barefoot. This was the difference between personal restriction and liberty, and I used every ploy to stretch the time of freedom between early spring and late autumn. When I reached school age, there was another separation of the year, with 180 days in the classroom and the other, slight majority of days divided up among weekends, three months of vacation in the summer, and ten more days in the heart of winter.

I was always aware of these various and overlapping parts of my calendar, but they faded into relative insignificance when compared with Christmas. This all-too-brief holiday brought a relaxation of duties, the peak of excitement, the maximum concentration of love and affection, the epitome of familial integration, and the realization or frustration of hopes and expectations. This was also the time when we were most likely to consider how well our daily lives and customs measured up to the heavenly standards that we were supposed to absorb in church, at school, and from our more devout relatives and friends. During this time of rest and contemplation, the success or failure of our crops and even the personal joys or sorrows that had befallen us were judged to be God's will, and we wondered how much our own behavior had affected the results.

Throughout the year, Daddy and I were on the lookout in our woods for a relatively rare wild red cedar that would make a good Christmas tree, one that was perfect in size and shape. It was something of a ceremony when we went out a few days before Christmas to bring it home. My father was meticulous about its quality, and if there were unsightly gaps anywhere in the foliage we would drill a small hole into the tree trunk and insert an extra limb or two. During our hunt for a tree, there was time to cut enough broom sedge that grew wild in the fields to make Christmas gifts for our kinfolks in town and to use for sweeping around our own fireplaces. Daddy taught me how to use a dull knife to strip away the slender leaves, beat a bundle of the remaining stalks to get rid of all the fluffy seedpods, and then bind them tightly together to make straw brooms.

Decorating our house for Christmas added to the excitement of the season. We children would paint different-colored magnolia leaves at school, and these were mixed with the green leaves and red berries of holly to decorate our mantelpiece, table-tops, and around the base of the tree. There was an enormous American holly tree in the middle of one of our fields, and since we and interlopers had long ago removed the lower leaves and berries, I would climb high enough with a hatchet or machete to send what we needed down to my waiting sisters and parents. My favorite way to get mistletoe, usually at the top of oak or pecan trees and on the ends of slender limbs, was to shoot into the clump and let the bullets or buckshot cut off some sprigs.

We made Christmas-tree decorations in our classrooms at school, and proudly presented them to our parents. The most common were long chains of circled and glued paper strips of different colors to be draped over the tree limbs, and these were supplemented with ropes of popcorn or cranberries strung on long slender threads. We contrived all kinds of dangling ornaments, either flat or three-dimensional, and affixed them to the limbs with small strings or hay wire. There was tinfoil in each package of cigarettes (my father smoked several packs a day), which we painstakingly cut into very narrow strips to use as tinsel, or "icicles."

All of us were proud to learn how to make a perfect five-pointed star with one scissor snip if the heavy paper was folded correctly, and then we covered it with tinfoil. Either this or an angel was mounted on top of our tree as the crowning ornament. Much later, when Rosalynn and I had a family of our own, someone gave us a really fancy store-bought star, and our children insisted on suspending it from the ceiling, to be raised or lowered each Christmas to match the exact height of succeeding trees. (We still leave the ornament hanging there all year, as a great reminder of past and future holidays.)

Even without electricity, the decorations could be beautiful. I believe the most admired tree we ever saw in Plains was a small holly cut by the family of one of my friends, perfectly shaped, covered with red berries, and strung just with threaded popcorn.

# 4

# Fireworks

★

One highlight of Christmas in Plains, now long forbidden by state law, was fireworks. Even in those early days, an ordinance prevented their sale inside the city limits, but temporary stands were within a few feet of all four entrances to town during the holidays, and they did a thriving business. A pack of twenty firecrackers cost a nickel, and we took great delight in finding different ways to explode them. One small firecracker under an empty tin can would propel it high into the air—the smaller the can, the farther it would go. We made a much longer-ranged projectile by placing a small rubber ball on top of a three-quarter-inch pipe after we dropped a firecracker inside. A shovelful of hot coals would serve to light the explosives for an hour or so, or sometimes slender sticks of slow-burning "punk" would come with a quantity of fire-works.

Cherry bombs or extra-large firecrackers, which cost a nickel each, were much more powerful, and their singular detonations could be heard all over town. They would blow a tin can to smithereens and dig a hole in the ground. Despite the stern warnings of our parents, we would light both regular firecrackers and cherry bombs and then throw them on the ground, often at each other's feet. Just once did I have one explode about two inches from my hand, and I had to suspend my arm in a sling for a few days, the broken skin on my purple fingers dressed with an antiseptic and bandages.

Roman candles were loaded with a dozen flaming projectiles, and were almost perfect for boys to twirl around and then shoot at each other. The girls and little children were usually satisfied with harmless sparklers. We might have one or two skyrockets, which were treated with great care because their flight was sometimes erratic and they could set fires where they landed.

There were explosions all around Plains on Christmas Eve and Christmas Day, but there was no equivalent New Year's celebration. Since we all went to bed every night shortly after dark, it would have been unthinkable to stay awake six more hours just to see midnight come. Later, when I was a teenager, my sisters and I spent a New Year's Eve night with my grandmother, and we decided to see why some people considered this to be a big event. Grandma agreed to wake us at midnight, and we went out on the front steps to see the years change. We were very disappointed.

All our "uptown" fireworks celebrations with our white friends in Plains faded into insignificance when compared with the importance of my black friends' fireball parties in Archery. Adults and children sewed handfuls of rags into tight little balls, and then gathered at night for the celebration. When the time came, the balls would be soaked in a bucket of kerosene and lit into flaming projectiles that could be flung high into the night sky. Everyone was careful to stay well away from any building, usually out in a nearby field, and each thrower was responsible for running to the landing place of his fireball so that no grass fires could spread into the nearby woodlands.

I tried it a couple of times, but didn't do well. I

thought it would be better to have a hay-wire handle, which would both protect my hand and give a slingshot effect to increase throwing range, but it seemed that the direct contact was an important, even crucial element of the game. The trick was to learn how to hold the burning rag ball long enough to throw it without having it burn one's fingers. Remembering that the flames and heat always went upward guided our bare hands to the bottom part of the ball.

Another unforgettable event concerning Christmas fireworks occurred in Plains, and still causes some embarrassment on the rare occasions when it is discussed. Our town marshal and some other men decided to have a little "harmless" fun on Saturday before the big day with a group of black citizens who customarily assembled in front of Roy Brannen's store. They cut a cylinder about four inches in diameter and a foot long from a stiff cardboard tube, which had been used as the shipping carton for fragile lamp chimneys. After stuffing it with cotton, the pranksters inserted a regular dynamite fuse of the kind that we used on the farm to remove stumps from new ground, and glued red wrapping paper around it, all to resemble an enormous firecracker.

Then they sneaked into the back of the grocery store, went up to the front door, lit the fuse, and threw the door open, and the marshal drew his arm back to throw the lighted "firecracker" out onto the sidewalk. In his excitement and haste, he let the artificial explosive slip from his hand, and it fell on the floor inside the store. There was a riot among the unsuspecting customers, clerks, and proprietor, and several counters and display cases were overturned as the store rapidly emptied. My neighbors out at Archery thought that divine justice was involved.

\*

The memories that surround Christmas are exceptionally vivid to me, perhaps because most of the year was devoted to routine and predictable work on the farm or at school, and the holidays were a time of surprise, relaxation, and fun.

A Christmas event in Archery that people still remember was caused by a sharp curve in the sandy U.S. highway in front of our house. One year, a few days before Christmas, I was standing near the barn with Jack Clark, and we heard and then saw a large truck approaching, traveling all too fast. When it reached the sharp turn, the truck leaned way over, the right wheels came up off the ground, and we expected it to turn completely on its side. Somehow, the driver was successful in righting his vehicle, but just as the tires settled back on the surface, they encountered the washboard ridges that always developed within a week or two after a motor grader scraped the road. The entire truck body came up a few inches and then dropped back down, but the back gate swung open, and the contents began pouring out as the truck disappeared in the distance.

With the farmers' market in Columbus still sixty miles farther west, the driver had dumped his cargo of holiday grapefruit from Florida along a half-mile stretch of road near our house. The driver never came back, and we always wondered how he felt when he arrived at his destination with an empty truck.

It is difficult now to imagine how precious an orange, an apple, or a tangerine was to the families in Archery. Just one or two such delicacies were often the entire harvest of gifts that a child could expect from Santa Claus. Now, within a few minutes, all the residents of the community were harvesting an almost unlimited quantity of fresh fruit into their tubs, baskets, and wagons. Except for the Carter family, none had ever tasted a grapefruit, and we were busy for a while answering questions about how they should be eaten. We soon learned that very few of our neighbors actually consumed more than the first sour bite, even after cooking failed to make them edible, and only the hungriest hogs were eager to get them.

Another exciting Christmas event was when a young black teenager climbed up on the Plains water tank, adjacent to the city hall, and threatened to commit suicide. Eighty feet above the ground, he rebuffed all inducements to descend from his high perch, and announced that he would not talk anymore and would jump if anyone tried to approach him. After discussing the situation, the town leaders decided to go to the hospital and get my mother. Everyone knew that she was a well-trained nurse, with at least a rudimentary knowledge of psychology, and was trusted within the black community.

When Mama arrived at the base of the tower, the men shouted up, "This is Miss Lillian Carter, and she wants to talk to you." Everyone became completely quiet, and Mama began speaking to the young man in a calm voice. Soon he was responding to her questions, and then Mama climbed about halfway up the ladder. After a while, she learned that the boy had gotten a severe whipping at home and was afraid of his mother's common-law husband, who had drunk too much moonshine on the holiday. She finally persuaded the boy to come down, but only after she agreed that everyone else would leave the area and that she would accompany him home with a sheriff's deputy to ensure that he would not be beaten again. We all thought Mama was a real heroine. She said, "Aw, he was just a boy that needed someone to pay attention to him."

★

In addition to going to Plains for school and to sell boiled peanuts during the summer days, I was also introduced to nightlife in Plains at an early age. My widowed grandmother Nina refused to be alone after dark, so one of her grandchildren was required to stay with her. My turn came on Fridays, as soon as I was old enough to use her telephone in case of an emergency. She lived right behind the Methodist church, and there was a nearby streetlight that stayed on until about nine o'clock. We children would sometimes play hide-and-seek, kick-the-can, and other games even an hour or two after sundown.

It was there that I met my first sweetheart, Eloise Ratliff, and where I suffered one of my life's greatest disillusionments. One night, as Christmas approached, I was babbling away about what Santa Claus might bring, and some of the older boys began to ridicule me about my foolish confidence in a fairy tale. After that, I still clung to my beliefs as long as I could, even though I harbored doubts, and don't ever recall asking my parents for the truth, which is sometimes best not known.

This was not the only occasion on which I refused to acknowledge that I might have been deceived.

At Christmas season, we children became fascinated with snow. We saw pictures of Santa at the North Pole, flying through the sky behind his reindeer with white flakes swirling around the sleigh loaded with gifts. The Katzenjammer Kids and other characters in the funny papers were always building snowmen and having snowball battles. We actually saw a scattering of snowflakes a few times during our early years, and the first excited cries of "It's snowing! It's snowing!" would instantly empty our house or the classrooms. In my grandmother's house there was a small, clear globe filled with liquid that, if shaken, would cause white flakes to swirl around for a few moments. This helped us imagine how real snow would be.

Gussie Abrams Howell (Miss Abrams), who was the chief nurse where my mother served on duty, was also my godmother. One December, she was preparing to escort a patient to Cleveland, Ohio, for psychiatric treatment, and she came by our house to talk to Mama before leaving on the trip. She asked us children what we wanted her to bring us as a Christmas present, and after consulting with each other we shouted, "A snowball!" We waited eagerly for Miss Abrams to return. She brought us an enormous white marble. We kept it carefully on a shelf in our front room, and I don't remember how long it was before any of us would admit that it was not a real petrified snowball.

# 5

# Religion

★

Although we recognized the religious foundation of Christmas, there was a limit on how much time we spent in church during the holidays. For instance, we knew that families in some communities attended special worship services when Christmas Day did not come on Sunday, but this was not our custom during my childhood.

As far as the white people of Plains were concerned, the role of our three churches was gently but carefully circumscribed. Whether Baptist, Methodist, or Lutheran, our families did not expect the pastor, deacons, stewards, or other congregation leaders to interfere in private or personal affairs or to interrupt regular schedules, except to offer help or comfort when needed and to preside over religious services, funerals, and weddings.

Our family never missed worship services on Sunday mornings. My father was both a deacon and the teacher of junior boys, ages nine through twelve, so we went to Sunday school every week at Plains Baptist Church and always stayed on first and third Sundays for the morning sermon (which was expected to end at precisely noon). Then Daddy would drive by the Suwannee store, where we picked up a copy of the *Atlanta Constitution* before returning home. Unlike some of the other church members, who were either more dedicated to extra Bible study or lived nearer Plains, we usually did not return for the Sunday-evening services.

The theologies and liturgies of the three congregations were almost indistinguishable, and believers moved easily from one to another because of marriage or perhaps some disagreement with other members. These exchanges did not detract from our devout and unshakable Protestant beliefs. We always had a special Sunday-school lesson and a sermon about the birth of Christ on the Sunday nearest Christmas, and for a couple of weeks we selected only carols in our hymnbooks. But it would have been considered inconvenient to the congregation if an extra service were scheduled when December 25 fell on a weekday.

I attended classes from the first grade all the way through high school in Plains, and there we received additional instruction in the religious meaning of the Christmas season, not only about the birth of Jesus but also about the subsequent impact of this event on the world. At some time during the last week before Christmas vacation, each of our classes was expected to perform a brief pageant in chapel (our daily assembly) that explained the different facets of this story. We enjoyed these performances, because some of those by the smallest kids were hilarious as the wise men, the innkeeper, Mary, Joseph, the shepherds, and the artificial animals intertwined their experiences, often with impromptu lines.

We also had to draw names so that each student would give a present to one other in the class, and on the last day before the holidays we would exchange gifts. There was a lot of good-natured teasing when our temporary "partner" was an unattractive classmate or someone we were known to dislike. The Christmas spirit was violated when we ostentatiously disavowed any special attachment to the equally mortified recipient of our gift, but I don't recall anyone's refusing to give or accept a Christmas present.

It would have been ridiculous in those days for anyone in our community, or the state of Georgia, to think that the dedicated religious services that were held every day in the public school might violate in any way the First Amendment to the U.S. Constitution. We accepted that one major role of our teachers was to be intimately involved in religious instruction. After all, we were all Christians or—if we were still too young to have personally accepted Christ as Saviour—these observances of the season were preparation for that almost inevitable decision. There were a few parents, well known to all believers, who did not attend church services, but they were visited at least once a year by a team of men who would explain the "plan of salvation" and urge them to be redeemed. The school programs about Christmas were at least as dedicated as those in the churches, and maybe even more effective, because they reached every child, not just the churchgoers.

★

Although I spent almost every free hour with my black friends, there was total racial segregation concerning both worship and education, so I was only slightly informed and not at all involved in what they did at school or in religious services.

The black worshipers always had at least six churches in the small town of Plains, and a few more were located in the nearby rural communities. There was not a schoolhouse for the children in Archery, and since school buses were only for white students and the black families had no automobiles, all their schooling and worship services had to be within walking distance. Public-school classes in Archery were held in small rooms in homes, or scattered about in the various corners of St. Mark AME Church.

Because of Bishop Johnson's Home and Industrial College, some of the black children enjoyed a rare oasis of apparent prosperity and hope in this special place. Private-school instruction was available for a few local children at the college, but most of this higher level of education was for boys and girls who lived elsewhere and came to Archery to stay in the dormitory. Everyone in the community used the excellent library that Bishop Johnson had accumulated, including the Carters and the family of the Seaboard Airline section foreman.

Our family usually attended church services at St. Mark AME Church only about once a year, when the bishop invited us to hear him take over preaching duties from the regular pastor and a special choir came down from one of the colleges in Atlanta. But I knew from my friends that, in contrast to the white churches in Plains, religious observances in Archery were much more prevalent at Christmastime, and usually included some kind of program for several days or nights at St. Mark's.

One of the favorite events was the choir singing *a cappella,* using shaped notes and inherited rhythms to bring the ancient hymns to life. The choirmaster was John Raven, Sr., the father of my two close friends Johnny and Milton, and there were regular practice sessions in their home throughout the year so the choristers could provide special music in the church and college. What my black playmates remember most vividly about these performances was that the bishop's oldest son, Alvan, would sit in the back pew, surrounded by his friends, and improvise alternate lyrics to the hymns being sung from the pulpit. One of his favorites, which still brings loud laughter from his friends, was during "Oh, there's sunshine, blessed sunshine in my soul"; Alvan always substituted "moonshine" for the key word. He must have had a good voice, because later he sang in the men's choir at Harvard University.

There were differences between how the black families and we observed the holidays. Their big moments on Christmas Day were not in their homes, but at St. Mark's church and directly across the road and railroad at Bishop Johnson's college. There was always a large pine tree in both places, with dozens of small presents attached to the limbs.

Each child in the community had a gift at the church, but there were two provisos, one of which was very troubling to most of the children. They would have to give a recitation of some kind just before they received their gifts. Most of the orations were just a single Bible verse or one couplet from a poem, but a few of the more ambitious children would show off with a carefully crafted speech or poem of their own. The other requirement, which

lasted all year for the college students, was to walk up and down the railroad track gathering chunks of coal that had fallen from the many steam engines that passed through Archery, to keep the church and college warm during the winter.

In the small college auditorium, Bishop Johnson always provided a second gift of some kind, this time for both adults and children. One year, for instance, it was a small tablet and a pencil. Mr. Watson's children were the only white people there to receive a present. The little children were thankful to Santa Claus, but the adults generally assumed that all the Christmas presents came not from the North Pole but from the great man in our own community. With the exception of these ceremonial affairs, the black children usually spent the day going from one house to another, enjoying each other's playthings and having at least rudimentary refreshments at each place.

# 6

# Christmas at Our House

★

One of the big things in the homes of Plains families was the preparation of special food for the Christmas holidays. Daddy's sister, Ethel, would bake several kinds of cakes, including pound cake, carrot, caramel, chocolate, angel food, coconut, pineapple upside down, and our favorite, Japanese fruitcake. Aunt Ethel always made sure that we had an adequate supply of desserts, and I presume now that Daddy paid her for them.

My mother wasn't much of a cook, although when she was not on nursing duty she was perfectly capable of providing our regular meals of fried chicken, fish, quail, cornbread, biscuits, and all kinds of meats and vegetables from our fields and garden. One dessert that Mama did make was ambrosia, and we children looked forward each year to punching nail holes in the "eyes" of coconuts, drinking the juice, and then bursting them open and grating the extracted chunks of meat.

I guess it would be more accurate to say that Mama never liked to cook, and welcomed my father into the kitchen whenever he was willing. He was always the one who prepared battercakes or waffles for breakfast, and he would even make a couple of Lane cakes for Christmas. Since this cake recipe required a strong dose of bourbon, it was just for the adult relatives, doctors, nurses, and other friends who would be invited to our house for eggnog.

Daddy gave the same enthusiasm and dedication to his food preparation as he did to the operation of our entire farm, and his preparation of eggnog was really a big deal. He produced a very large bowl of it each Christmas, which required an enormous amount of carefully coordinated work. Daddy made us children feel important by inviting us to help him in this great endeavor.

Dozens of egg whites and quarts of cream had to be whipped into simultaneous stiffness, with sugar and whiskey being added slowly and carefully. As the time approached for guests to arrive, all of them warned to be punctual, we would be madly beating the ingredients in smaller bowls while Daddy orchestrated the proper mixing, to assure that the eggnog was as stiff and erect as possible when served. His goal was a minimum amount of loose liquid in the bottom of the special glasses. This delicious mixture was served with a sprinkling of ground nutmeg on top of each drink. A small amount, without the whiskey, was set aside for us children, and Daddy always saved a small pitcherful for Jack and Rachel Clark. Not being included in the party, they would either drink it in the kitchen or, most of the time, take it down to their house to enjoy.

### Earl Carter's Chistmas Recipe for Eggnog

Ingredients, for each quart of whiskey or rum:

> 3 dozen eggs
> 3 cups of sugar
> 3 pints of cream
> ground nutmeg

Separate the eggs, and beat the yolks until stiff, adding sugar and whiskey. Keep everything cool while you beat the egg whites and cream. Then carefully blend all together and serve, with a sprinkling of nutmeg on top.

*Serves 32*

Church congregations dominated the superficial rules of politics of our region, so ours was officially a completely dry county, but this didn't interfere in any way with the serving of spirituous libations to those who wanted them. Daddy had inherited winemaking paraphernalia from his father, and each year produced several gallons from grapes, black cherries, peaches, or apples. Anyone could buy Atlantic ale at the plant where ice was made near Muckalee Creek, and the county bootlegger lived just west of there, on the outskirts of Americus, and only nine miles from Plains. Identifiable customers would drive into his yard, stop under a wooden canopy that seemed to be a carport, purchase almost any kind of bonded whiskey, and circle around behind his house to return to the main road. They would then proceed to their homes or to a regular evening of entertainment in Americus at the American Legion, VFW, Elks Club, or, for a few wealthier and socially elite families, the Country Club.

In addition, there were a number of moonshiners in the area, jackleg operators with small, easily concealed stills on wooded streams. These were most often poor farmers who were attempting to supplement their sparse income by turning some of their corn crop into alcohol. The quality of their 'shine was doubtful, and some of them saved money by using lead pipes instead of copper tubing in the distillation process. There were frequent articles in the state newspapers about lead-poisoning epidemics that would break out, often with several fatalities blamed on the bad whiskey. I remember two times when we boys found a still in some of my father's most remote swamps, and he reported them to the revenuers for destruction.

The most common source of "good" spirits was a small group of elite distillers who were well known to produce alcohol of high quality. One of them lived about a mile from our house. Many citizens who were not teetotalers highly regarded these responsible moonshiners, perhaps because they were willing to be jailed every now and then, when the sheriff or revenue agents moved in to make a symbolic arrest. The prearranged sentences were fairly brief, and we could tell from our front porch when our neighbor was back home from the penitentiary because we could see a steady stream of headlights going to his home, on what everyone in Archery called Moonshine Road. Almost invariably, my parents and their friends drank bonded whiskey from the county bootlegger, but as a friendly gesture they would accept a quart of our neighbor's product when he came by with an exceptionally fine sample.

My father was also an expert at preparing the special holiday meats that used up the aftermath of hog-killing time. One of his favorites was what we called sousemeat, a conglomeration of feet, ears, faces, and other parts that were cleaned thoroughly, boiled into a homogeneous glutinous consistency, seasoned heavily, and then formed into a large loaf. Daddy was very proud of this, and took pleasure in presenting it to friends and relatives who came to see us. We children rather suspected that it reduced the number of our holiday visitors. Predictably, Daddy would repeat the old joke, "There are two things you never want to see being made: sousemeat and laws."

★

As the big day approached, we children went through a gamut of imagined gifts that might be ours on Christmas morning, finally honing our lists down to a reasonable balance between high expectations and the cautionary responses of our parents, designed to deflate our hopes. Then we would mail our letters to Santa Claus at the North Pole, hoping that he would be more generous than we were being led to expect. Not quite understanding the interrelationships, we nevertheless used maximum propaganda around the house.

"Mama, if I just had one of those little Red Racer wagons in the Sears catalogue, I could haul wood to the house, water to the field hands, and vegetables from the garden. During peanut season, it would make it easy to bring some peanuts home from the field so I could boil them to sell." My real visions were of A.D. and me pulling each other back and forth around the farm, and flying down a steep hill together.

There was no chance that we might intimidate our parents, or beg successfully for particular gifts.

The process of our expressing hopes and their dashing them was strangely routine and impersonal, our goal being to obtain as much as possible for ourselves and theirs to minimize disappointment when we didn't get what we wanted. At least for us children, Baby Jesus was not involved in this important dialogue.

It didn't seem right—at least to her—for Mama to have to cook a complete breakfast on Christmas morning, so we always had just sausage, biscuits, and jelly—a custom that we Carters have maintained for seventy years. This menu could be prepared the afternoon or evening before, kept in either the icebox or the warming compartment of the woodstove, and heated up quickly. In fact, we rarely even built a fire in the big cooking stove on Christmas Day. When we didn't eat dinner with some of our kinfolks, Mama would warm up leftover fried chicken or we would eat country-ham, pimiento-cheese, or peanut-butter-and-jelly sandwiches. What served as our "microwave" in those days was the kerosene stove, which could be lit instantly and provided either an oven or two grills.

One of the great crises of our childhood was

when our baby sister, Ruth, found a way to open a valve and suck out some of the kerosene. I remember that she turned a dark color before Mama could induce her to vomit by sticking a finger down her throat while Daddy held her upside down.

★

Since our house was always cold in the winter, the fireplace in the front room controlled the official beginning of Christmas morning. We were absolutely prohibited from entering this sacrosanct place until after Daddy had gotten up and built a good fire. Several times during the night, one of us would go into our parents' bedroom, to be met with a stern "Go back to bed! It's just two o'clock." Finally, about an hour before daylight, we would hear Daddy get up and replenish the fire in the round woodstove in their room, and we'd rush in there and put on our clothes as the chill slowly dissipated. In the meantime, Daddy would go to the front room and build a good blaze in the fireplace, which we had carefully let die down the previous night so Santa could come in without burning his britches.

After an excruciating wait, we would be given permission to dash into the front room. The cookies and milk we had left out for our distinguished guest would be gone, and his presents would be in our assigned places in front of the hearth. Our parents were experts at convincing us that we would get "some fruit and maybe some clothes that you've been needing." What we dreaded most was underwear (BVDs) and socks, so our reaction was genuine pleasure when one or two toys or some books were also there. My sisters would almost always get a "Bi-Low" doll. Once, after a good crop year, Gloria and I both got bicycles.

I don't remember much about gifts to my parents, who never seemed to expect anything and usually insisted that "Christmas is for children." Except one year, after Mama had nursed members of a black family and refused to charge them for her services, they delivered what turned out to be her favorite gift of the Christmas season. It was made by Felton Shelton, who lived on our farm and wove baskets of white-oak strips.

The present was what Felton called, for some unexplained reason, a "sky mop" (scour mop?). He drilled nine holes in a block of wood about eighteen inches long, the center one at an angle for insert-ing a long handle. Then he twisted corn shucks and wedged them into the other holes, making an almost indestructible scrubber that could be used to apply the caustic Red Devil lye to our floors. Mama did this at least a couple of times a year to keep bedbugs and other insidious vermin out of our house.

My most common request to Santa Claus was for two or three books, and I would prepare my choices very carefully. Sometimes I had suggestions from my mother or our school superintendent, Miss Julia Coleman, but most of the time I would search through the book section of the Sears, Roe-buck catalogue and make my choices. Above all my other requests, this was the one that was most certain to be honored, because Mama was always encouraging me to read as much as possible.

The year I was eight years old, I was amazed to find a large cardboard box under the Christmas tree with a tag on it that said, "Love from Miss Abrams." She was the same head nurse who brought us the marble "snowball" from Cleveland. When I opened the gift, I found twenty-six leather-bound books, including the complete works of Victor Hugo and a twenty-volume set of *The Outline of Knowledge*. Mama eased my concern by telling me that I could take a few years to read through the entire collection.

The next year, we had our usual Christmas morning, and once again my most cherished gifts were some books that I had wanted. During the day, however, both my sister Gloria and I developed red spots on our faces, began to cough, and had itching eyes and runny noses. It took Mama only a brief glance to announce that we had measles, which we all knew was making the rounds of the Plains community. We listened to her stern admonition about going blind if we strained our eyes or exposed them to bright light. Her prescription was like a prison sentence: in addition to the aspirin and cough syrup, we had to stay in bed in a darkened room.

I wanted to obey Mama, but the new books on the table were too much of a temptation to resist. After an hour or so, I eased up a window shade, got one of my new books, and lay on the floor by the window to read, hidden behind the bed. It was almost inevitable that Mama would catch me, and then she searched the room, removed all the reading material, and gave me a stern warning that

Daddy would administer a fearsome punishment if I disobeyed her again.

My most memorable Christmas morning was when I found, as had been predicted dismally by my parents, just two oranges, some English walnuts, dried raisins, and a pair of trousers. Trying not to appear frantic or disappointed, I searched all around the tree, and attempted to control my trembling lips and to hold back tears. I considered myself too old to cry. After a few moments, Daddy said, "Sometimes I think old Santa might leave something out in the yard." I looked out of the living-room window and didn't see anything, and then ran back to my room. There, outside, with her reins tied to a tree limb, was a Shetland pony! I dashed out of the house, and ten minutes later A.D. and I were taking turns in the saddle. I named her Lady, and for the next ten years she was a most wonderful companion.

Our family usually exchanged and relished our gifts early in the morning, and then traveled around to visit some of the other members of our family, either in nearby Plains or among my mother's folks in Richland, eighteen miles to the west, finally arriving at the place chosen that year for our big

noon meal. After that, we would return home for a remarkable afternoon of total leisure, similar to what we usually enjoyed on Sundays but without any restraints against things like shooting guns or playing cards. The farm would be almost completely devoid of black neighbors, who would be visiting friends or relatives. Their travels by foot or on wagons took longer, of course, than ours by automobile. Except for the unavoidable chores of caring for animals and toting in water, firewood, and stove wood, no one was expected to have any duties.

*

The separation from my black friends on Christmas Day felt somewhat strange. For this one occasion, blood kinship and economic circumstances controlled our family's activities. When we did encounter someone on the farm early in the morning, there was a great competition to be the first to claim a present from the other person by shouting, "Christmas gift!" This was often done at a great distance, to avoid the obligation that fell on the one who didn't cry out first. Whenever I sneaked up and got ahead of A.D. or one of my other playmates, though, they would reply, "Well, gimme it," in an effort to turn the tables. Another response was, "I'se jes fixin t'say it!" In fact, though, it was just a game. We realized that they had nothing to give, and Mama always had a small present for each child on the farm.

We Carter children expected and usually received some nice presents on Christmas, and sometimes it was embarrassing to compare mine with those of my black playmates. There was no doubt they also believed in Santa Claus, but their expectations were much lower. With annual incomes of just three hundred dollars or so to buy food, clothing, medical care, and all the other necessities of life for an entire family, their Christmases lacked any such luxuries as store-bought toys or presents. But it wasn't long before we were all sharing whatever toys we had, with A.D. asserting his completely equal rights, "All right, Jimmy, now it's my turn!"

Usually, the black children had individual shoe-boxes labeled with their names, carefully saved from one season to another. These would be placed side by side near the fireplace, and an outstanding Christmas morning would bring an orange or an apple

and some raisins, dried on the stems and with seeds intact. (Even for many of my white classmates, this gift of fruit was all they could expect.) A little boy might get a toy made by his father, and a girl usually expected a homemade doll, with corn shucks or wheat straw making up its main structure. Whether Christmas or not, each boy had his own gallon syrup can with a small hole punched in each end and a piece of hay wire running through the holes and formed into a pulling loop. Filled with sand, these little "automobiles" or "wagons" could be pulled behind us for hours. It was rare that joy from a store-bought toy could exceed the long-term pleasure from those we contrived on the farm.

When I was big enough to make a sale and keep records in an account book, I worked as a clerk in Uncle Buddy's Plains Mercantile Company on Saturdays and for a few days before Christmas, so I often knew what presents some of the other children would get from Santa. One of my most poignant experiences each holiday season was to watch a few of the poor parents search through a long table that was covered with special toys, none of which cost more than a dime. After they had bought the cheapest food and other necessities of life, with perhaps a piece of fruit for each of their children, they would come to the front of the store to spend a few cents on frivolous things.

I would help them choose between the tiny tin or celluloid figurines, coloring books, small boxes of crayons, cloth bags containing a few marbles, wooden tops, or artificial watches, both of whose hands would rotate together as the winding stem was turned. The table also held a few of the more expensive toys that were defective or damaged. In these families without money, the religious aspects of the season had little competition from the material world, except for the special pleasure of a day or so on which there was no work in the fields or woodlands and family visits might be possible.

One of my childhood Archery friends, Addie Wright, remembers receiving an unusually nice store-bought doll once, with a white face of course, but with a porcelain head that was already cracked. Almost seventy years later, she surmises that her mother bought it at Plains Mercantile Company at a discount, and she still recalls how, although she kept it in its box and nursed it with extreme tenderness and care, the doll's head shattered the first time it received a slight bump. After some long discussions with her sisters, they finally decided to bury the remains with an appropriate funeral service. She told me, "I can still take you to the gravesite."

★

One gift from Santa Claus that was almost inevitable for a farm boy like me was a Daisy air rifle. This was the first step toward ultimate manhood: to master the necessary skills and safety rules of using firearms for hunting. I don't even remember when I received my first Red Rider model, but it seems that it was mine even before I was strong enough to cock the lever by myself. After Daddy was certain that I was thoroughly familiar with the weapon and knew the safety rules and basic courtesies expected among hunters, I was free—even encouraged—to use my gun when and where I chose.

In the process of growing up, I graduated to higher-powered air guns, a .22-caliber rifle, and then a bolt-action .410-gauge shotgun. It was natural that, both in town and on the farms, I listened attentively when the grown men were talking about hunting. White folks almost invariably discussed birds, and black men concentrated on raccoons, opossums, rabbits, and squirrels. The two birds sought in those days were mourning doves, shot while flying into fields to feed on grain or peanuts left over from the harvest, and bobwhite quail, which were always called "pottages" (partridges) or merely "birds." If someone said, "I'm going bird-hunting," it meant quail. This was a sport of great sophistication, involving enough nuances about game, dogs, shotguns, hunting techniques, marksmanship, habitats, and favorite recipes to sustain long conversations during all twelve months of the year.

Since shooting a gun on Sunday was inconceivable, the hunters in our area cherished Christmas (sometimes stretched to three days) as a prime time to shoot bobwhite quail. One of the things I wanted even more than Santa Claus's gifts was an invitation from Daddy to accompany him on at least one of these adventures. We always had two or three good bird dogs, and Jack Clark helped with the training of these pointers and setters. When I was too small to carry my own shotgun, I was sometimes permitted to tag along with Jack Clark, observing how he handled the dogs and listening to his running commentaries.

Quail-hunting with my father would be an acknowledgment of responsibility and maturity that I knew would not come lightly. Daddy began taking me with him on dove shoots when I was about six years old, to spot incoming flights and to mark and pick up those he had killed. But he resisted my entreaties to accompany him to hunt quail. This was considered to be a man's sport, highly sophisticated and potentially dangerous, with hunters close together, quick movements, and unpredictable shooting.

Between the middle of November and February, my father tried to go out for a hunt whenever possible, but he worked very hard every day, harder than most other men I knew, and the times were rare when Daddy could spend an entire afternoon with his gun and dogs. It was a special event when this did happen and he went hunting with one of his friends who shared his love of the sport. A third hunter was considered to be a danger during the excitement, when a covey of about a dozen birds erupted from their hiding place with an explosive sound. Children or any onlookers were excluded, because they were in the way and also uneducated in the ancient niceties and customs.

One Christmas, when I was about ten years old, we had returned home after having dinner with our kinfolks, and I saw Daddy putting on his leather snake-proof leggings and his hunting jacket. "Lillian," he called, "I'm going hunting in the fields behind the house, maybe with Mr. Watson." He looked down at my imploring eyes, hesitated a few moments, and added, "Hot, do you want to go with me, if Mr. Watson can't go?" I almost fainted with excitement and forgot all about Santa Claus and gifts. Mama and I scurried around until I was as well dressed as possible for protection against snakes and briars. By then, it turned out that our neighbor was free to hunt, but Daddy decided to bend his rules and let me tag along, although not carrying a gun.

Throughout that memorable Christmas afternoon, I observed with great attention each order given the dogs, every safety precaution taken by the men with guns, and listened intently to their conversation about the habits of quail, the character of dogs, and the benefits of the hedgerows and fields through which we walked. I tried from my relatively low perspective to watch the dogs at every moment, and once or twice I was the first to notice when one of them froze into immobility, and shouted with a piping voice, "A point! A point!" Then I followed as closely as permitted behind my father and Mr. Watson as they hurried to the rear of the dog and walked forward with shotguns ready to fire, calling quietly to one dog, "Careful, Sport, careful," and at the same time making sure that our other dog, still dashing about in its own search for game, didn't inadvertently run into the site and flush the birds prematurely.

I knew to stay clear of any possible direction in which the guns might be fired, and to mark carefully where the first dead bird fell, often not noted exactly by the hunters when they whirled to follow later rising quail. Only after action at a particular place was over could the game be retrieved, and this was always the responsibility of the dogs.

I would report excitedly, "Daddy, the first bird is right over here, between the little dogwood and that bunch of broom sage." We would then approach the site but not walk into it, and Daddy would guide the dogs by calling, "Close in here, dead bird, dead, dead," until either Sue or Sport picked up the quail and carried it to him. When the hunt was over, we returned home at the end of an absolutely perfect Christmas Day—of gifts, family love, good food, and a total binding of myself to my father.

A completely different form of hunting that came every year during Christmastime was with the black men who lived in our community. For 365 days a year, Jack Clark had to care for the livestock and milk the cows, but during the few brief holidays even he would join other men on the farm in staying up all night and trying to grab some sleep during daylight hours. With no work in the fields or woods, this was a perfect time to hunt raccoons and opossums, and I was always eager to accept an invitation to join the men and their hounds. These were enjoyable expeditions because of the challenge and companionship involved, but quite serious in their purpose. The prospect of fresh meat to supplement the families' minimal diet was an attraction that warranted the relatively expensive feeding of a hound dog during the rest of the year. Daddy was not interested in this kind of sport, and we never owned a 'coon dog, but the workers on our place wanted me along because I was an accomplished and fearless tree-climber.

After the hunters assembled shortly before dark, there would be an extended discussion among the dog owners about which woodlands and swamps would be our destination, and then we would head in that direction, with the straining dogs held in check by ropes tied to their collars. When the dogs were finally released and dashed off into the woods, we usually squatted on our haunches or sat on a fallen log to listen to them. Every man recognized, without question, the voice of each dog, and understood the meaning of the yelps and howls as clearly as if the hounds were communicating in the English language over wireless radios. When one of the dogs "struck a trail," everyone knew immediately which one was in the lead, and understood that the owner of that dog had first choice of whatever game was captured.

We would usually wait where we were until the dogs were becoming too distant and we needed to follow, or until the quarry had been treed, at which time there would be a cacophony of frantic barking among all the dogs at the site. Carrying lanterns and one long multibattery flashlight, unlit to save batteries, we dashed through the limbs, briars, and brush and waded through water until we could join the dogs. Only then was the beam of our powerful flashlight focused on the high reaches of the tree, and we searched until the 'coon or 'possum finally looked down and its eyes were reflected—with surprising brilliance—to reveal its location.

The next task was to bring the animal to the ground, using a series of tactics, beginning with climbing the tree and shaking limbs and, if that was unsuccessful, reluctantly and as a last resort using a .22-caliber rifle bullet. For a smaller tree, we might just cut it down and depend on the dogs to catch whatever came down with it. Here again, circumstances could be quite different. A 'coon was a meticulously clean animal, and could often whip the dogs and escape to another tree. 'Possums were scavengers and needed to be fed clean food for a week or two before they were good to eat, and would often just curl up when they hit the ground and pretend to be dead.

The game was distributed as evenly as possible after the hunt was over, with the owner of the most successful dog getting first choice but sharing with the others, so that as many families as possible would have something special during the Christmas season. If someone came up short on this night, he would have privileged status for the next outing. Competition among the men and their hounds was intense, and there were hours of mostly good-natured arguments and debates during the night hunts and even in the fields throughout the year about such vital issues as which were the best breeds—walkers, blueticks, redbones, or black-and-tans. There were other interminable discussions about such things as how they should be trained and how vocal the best dogs should be.

# 7

# To a Broader World

*

I really began to shift my interests from Archery to nearby Plains about 1938, when I entered the senior grades in school, with academic affairs, basketball and baseball, church and school socials, and girls more and more on my mind. There was usually some kind of Christmas-night party for teenagers, and all of us boys expected to be paired with a steady girlfriend. I always had regular dates during my high school years, going steady at least for a few months with each of four different girls.

Since we were fascinated with jitterbugging in those days, Magnolia Springs was our favorite destination, with its jukebox and big dance floor. Although the pavilion could not be heated in wintertime and was usually closed, sometimes the dancing arena was opened at least this one night during the holidays. We stayed warm first with sweaters and then, later, with the frantic exercise of the acrobatic dancing. A typical date night would cost me a quarter— for a package of chewing gum, two Cokes, and a dime left over to pay my share in keeping the jukebox going.

When I was finally graduated from high school in 1941 and left home for college and the navy, I had a very clear commitment to attend Georgia Tech and then Annapolis, and to serve an entire career of thirty years in the U.S. Navy. I would then retire in Hawaii, or perhaps near Annapolis, in the unimaginably distant future. I had no way of knowing how few of my plans and ambitions were going to develop as expected. They all changed, but one thing would constantly be attracting me, something like the North Pole on a magnetic needle. The small town of Plains, with its few hundred people, would continue to be the focal point of my life, and Christmas was the time when I, along with those I loved, would always struggle to respond to that attraction.

8

# College Years

★

My class at the U.S. Naval Academy was on an accelerated schedule during the war, and four years of normal work were concentrated into just three years. However, we midshipmen were still given ten days of leave at Christmastime to visit our families at home. Although we were credited with a salary of sixty-five dollars a month, this amount was used for living expenses, including uniforms and other necessary purchases in the midshipmen's store. Any balance was credited to our accounts to use after graduation. For spending money we were limited strictly to four dollars each month the first year, seven the second year, and eleven dollars when we were first-classmen; my roommate and I spent most of this allowance on phonograph records.

I was always eager to get to Plains as quickly as possible when holidays came, but with so little money to spend most of us hitchhiked to avoid the cost of a train or bus ticket. I always found that motorists were generous to those of us in uniform, and we could make fairly good progress to our destinations, but there was a potentially faster route made available by a special dispensation of the Navy Department. We midshipmen were authorized to ride on any military airplanes that had an empty seat and happened to be going in our general direction. There was no way to predict when such an opportunity might arise, however, and it was quite possible that we could sit around the control tower at an air base for hours or the better part of a day. I lost an entire night of vacation during my second year at Annapolis, being bumped by first-classmen every time a potential ride was available.

The next summer, I was dating Miss Georgia Southwestern College, a beautiful girl named Annelle, and every night I drove my father's car the fifty-mile round trip to see her in Buena Vista, Georgia. But she was busy one night, and I had a blind date with Rosalynn Smith, a close friend of my younger sister, Ruth. I fell in love with her. Although we had grown up in the same community, I had never paid any attention to this girl, who was three years younger than I. On my last night of leave, after I took Annelle home, Rosalynn accompanied me to the train station to see me off for my trip back to Annapolis, on a ticket my father had bought.

I had no chance to see my new sweetheart until six months later, during Christmas vacation, and I was especially eager to get home. We heard that a few transport planes were leaving the Washington area and flying south, so I caught an automobile ride from Annapolis to Bolling Air Force Base, across the Potomac River from National Airport. After spending the night on the floor of a waiting room, I learned early the next morning, now two days before Christmas, that there was a plane going to Eglin Air Force Base, near Pensacola, Florida. Although this would still leave me more than 150 miles from home, I took the ride.

I was briefly distracted from my travel plans, because the air force had captured a Messerschmitt 109 and a Focke-Wulf 190 airplane from the Germans. American pilots were trained in them, and that day were conducting simulated combat trials in competition with our own P-38 Lightning and P-51 Mustang fighter planes. This was too fascinating to miss. As the only Naval Academy midshipman on the base, I was welcomed to the control tower to watch the aerial combat, and for an entire afternoon I almost forgot about Plains and Christmas.

But late in the day, when the exercises were over, I was approached by an air-force major, who was the most disfigured person I had ever seen. His face was one flaming-red scar, and he was missing his upper lip, nose, one of his ears, and part of his eyelids. He asked where I was trying to go. When I described the location of Plains, he said he was a B-24 bomber pilot and was taking his plane to a base near Atlanta. He offered me a ride. Although this wouldn't be much nearer Plains, there was regular bus service from there home.

The pilot asked me to join him in the cockpit, and after we took off he explained that he had been badly injured when his plane, with one engine damaged, had stalled on landing at a base in England. It had crashed and burned. He was scheduled to be discharged within a few weeks, and had been assured that the government would provide extensive cosmetic surgery. This Christmas would be his first visit home since his accident, and he was concerned about the reaction of his family, friends, and neighbors. I tried to reassure him in a roundabout way that his folks would realize that his injury was just superficial.

He examined his charts and soon said that we would be flying almost exactly over Turner Field, near Albany, Georgia, and asked if it was close to Plains. I replied that it was only thirty-five miles from home and that my parents often went shopping in the city. He got our home telephone number, made a radio call to the control tower, arranged for my parents to meet me, and prepared to go down.

It was a hair-raising experience for me. I had spent hours in the cockpits of navy planes as a midshipman, operating from land and in seaplanes, and was familiar with the basic procedure of heading into the wind and slowing almost to stalling speed before landing. Instead, we approached the landing strip at high speed, leveled off just as our wheels touched the ground, and then struggled to stop the plane before we reached the end of the runway.

After I thanked the pilot and was leaving the plane, one of the crew members whispered, "We'll never stall out while the major is at the controls."

As I waited the few minutes before my parents arrived and watched the *Liberator* take off and head north, I prayed that the pilot would have as good a Christmas visit as I was expecting. Since then, I have often thought about this Good Samaritan, and wondered if my prayers were answered.

*

These college years were a time of transition for me, having always been a boy enjoying Christmas within my parents' home. Now I was a young man considering for the first time a life with a possible family of my own. Even though my two sisters were grown up and our little brother, Billy, was approaching eight, our family tried to maintain the Christmas routine as much the same as ever. But it was obvious that Rosalynn and I were obsessed with each other, and I was not interested in the town's holiday customs or in visits among relatives. All I really wanted was to be with my sweetheart every possible moment during my time at home.

On the last day of my leave, I asked Rosalynn to marry me, and was taken aback when she turned me down. I headed back to the Naval Academy in despair, despite her promise to reconsider after she had spent two more years in college, to fulfill a promise made to her father on his deathbed. I persisted with my proposal when she came to visit me on Lincoln's Birthday, and she finally changed her mind. We were married in the Plains Methodist Church a month after I received my commission as an ensign. We returned to Plains for the following Christmas as man and wife, from our home in Norfolk, Virginia, where I was assigned to duty after being graduated from Annapolis.

# 9

# Christmas in the Navy

★

Rosalynn relished her independence as a navy wife, away from Plains and the influence of her family, and with almost total control of our family's affairs, but our memories of those early years of navy life are not very pleasant. What she remembers most vividly is being alone and pregnant. I was at sea almost all the time, so she was responsible for finding an apartment, buying food, paying the bills, and trying to save a few dollars. My salary was three hundred dollars a month; out of this we always bought a fifty-dollar war bond, my food bill on the ship was fifty-four dollars, and our rent was ninety-two dollars. I spent some off-duty hours in the woodshop on the navy base, and we managed slowly to accumulate rudimentary furniture and household supplies. Since we didn't have an automobile, our only transportation cost was bus and streetcar fare, for me to come home and back to the ship and for my wife to go shopping.

Rosalynn and I spent every possible moment together when I was off the ship, and, like the other young couples, we didn't want to share those precious hours with other dwellers in the same apartment complex. While the men were at sea, however, the navy wives would spend some time together and share responsibilities for shopping and babysitting. We rarely went to church near our apartment, but when I got off duty on Sunday mornings I would try to attend an early-morning church service on the navy base—either Protestant or Catholic, whichever one let me get home quickest.

We had our first son, Jack, in 1947, a year after we were married, and two other sons, Chip and Jeff, came along during the next five years. Each was born in a different navy hospital. All this time, while I was first serving on old experimental battleships and later in submarines, we tried to get back to Plains whenever possible, at least for Christmas. But I was never senior enough to have priority among the officers. This meant that we were at home in

Plains for only two of the seven holidays, and the other years I had a good chance of having to spend Christmas morning on my ship.

Rosalynn and the children would try to pretend that either the day before or the day after Christmas was the proper time for Santa Claus to come to our home and gifts to be exchanged. Usually, our captain was nice enough to permit a Christmas party on board, so we duty officers could invite our families to enjoy a tree and some festivities with us on the ship. On a few occasions during those years, either in the battleship's mess area or between the forward torpedo tubes of a submarine, I would meet with some others to read the Bible story of Jesus' birth.

My most traumatic holiday season was also the only time that Rosalynn and I were widely separated. I completed training as a submariner in December 1948 and was assigned to the USS *Pomfret* (SS 391), deployed out of Pearl Harbor, Hawaii. This was one Christmas season that I spent traveling, by land, air, and sea.

We had purchased our first automobile, a Studebaker Commander, and we drove from submarine school in New London, Connecticut, to Plains, where I left Rosalynn and our son, Jack, and proceeded on to Los Angeles. I made arrangements to load our car on a transport ship to be delivered to us a few months later, and caught a navy plane to Hawaii to report for duty. Almost immediately, during the last week in December, the *Pomfret* left for a four-month cruise to the Western Pacific, a lone submarine that would be conducting antisubmarine-warfare training exercises with surface ships of Australia, Great Britain, and the United States.

Shortly after leaving port, we ran into one of the most fearsome storms that had been seen in the Pacific for more than twenty years. We heard on our radio that several ships were sunk, and the rough seas made life miserable on the *Pomfret,* which was one of the standard submersibles deployed during World War II. We could operate underwater only for relatively limited periods, maybe a full day creeping along very slowly but only thirty minutes at top speed, while using power from our batteries. To recharge them, we had to cruise on the surface with our diesel engines running, and the tremendous waves required us to recirculate the same air, filled with diesel fumes, cigarette smoke, and obnoxious human odors. I vomited constantly for four days, finding a little relief only when I was on duty topside with the cold and clean waves and spray breaking over me.

Routinely, all submarines at sea in the Pacific had to report by radio to Pearl Harbor headquarters every eight hours, so that officials could monitor the status of each ship. The submarine would be called from the shore stations if no timely report was received, and after another eight hours of silence it was assumed that there was a serious problem. Our radio-transmission system was destroyed in the heavy weather, and we were unable to check in as required, but we could still receive the increasingly urgent calls that were coming in to us. Then we heard the ultimate message: "USS *Pomfret* (SS 391) is presumed lost at sea about six hundred miles south of Midway Island. All ships and planes should be on the lookout for floating debris." We knew, of course, that we were safe, but we were distressed to realize that our families were grieving about our presumed deaths.

Our captain decided to depart from our original orders to travel directly to China, and we turned toward Midway at maximum speed. We arrived there about fifty hours later, severely battered but safe, and the welcome news was transmitted to the outside world. It was not until almost four months later that I learned that Rosalynn, back in Plains, had not been notified of the *Pomfret*'s tragic fate.

*

On the Christmas days when I was off duty, Rosalynn and I tried to re-create the family customs that we remembered from our childhood, with a decorated tree, gifts, and perhaps a Bible reading from Luke's beautiful account of the first Christmas. Although we were always thankful to be together with our own small family, we usually managed to warm and enliven the day with telephone calls back to our folks in Plains. Also, we almost always had an apartment near other navy families, so our boys had plenty of children with whom to enjoy their toys. On three occasions we spent Christmas in the Northeast and had real snow during the holidays, with sleds and snowmen. Although I had seen snow a few times while at Annapolis and when my submarine was operating out of Seattle, Washington, this was my first time to enjoy it with my own family.

It was a totally different and delightful experience to observe Christmas as parents, with our little children anticipating Santa Claus. Rosalynn followed her mother's custom of baking an array of cakes and cookies in advance. She mostly concentrated on cookies, so the children could join in by cutting them into interesting shapes and sprinkling colored sugar granules on the surfaces.

For Christmas dinner we had her family's traditional old-fashioned banquet—either baked chicken or turkey with dressing, cranberry sauce, sweet-potato soufflé, rice, and green beans, usually topping it off with the cookies, cake, and ambrosia. We always had a tree of some kind, and I remember how insistent our boys were that they orchestrate the decorating. We had enough lights and ornaments, but they were necessarily concentrated on the lower limbs, as high as little arms could reach. The decorations were strangely distorted, but the tree was ours—and beautiful to us. For the Christmas story, we used children's books instead of the adults' Bible, and tried to impress on our little boys the real meaning of the holiday.

# 10

# Back Home in Georgia

★

I enjoyed my time in the navy and made rapid advancement, but my father was found to have pancreatic cancer in July 1953, and I took two weeks of unused leave and went home to Plains to be with my family. Rosalynn and our children stayed in Schenectady, New York, where I was senior officer of a crew of two dozen men preparing the propulsion system for the USS *Sea Wolf,* being built by General Electric at the same time Westinghouse was working on the USS *Nautilus.* These would be the first two nuclear-powered submarines, and there could not have been any better assignment for a young naval officer.

While at home, I spent as much time as possible at my father's bedside, knowing that he and I could have only a few more days together. I talked to a steady stream of people who came to the house, eager to express their prayers and good wishes but also to let me know how Daddy's personal and anonymous generosity had changed their lives. These were about an equal number of black and white citizens, most of whom I had never known or had forgotten during the twelve years I had been away. I was overwhelmed by the diversity and significance of my father's life in this small community, and I began to compare my own life with his. During the long drive back to Schenectady after the funeral, I decided to resign from the navy, to my own surprise as well as Rosalynn's. She and I had a furious argument about this shocking change in our family's future, but I was determined to return to Plains.

In October, having been discharged from my official duties, Rosalynn, Jack (six), Chip (three), Jeff (one), and I drove home in our Plymouth station wagon. Rosalynn hardly spoke a word to me, still furious because of my decision to leave the navy. We stopped briefly in Washington, so I could thank Senator Richard Russell, who, as chairman of the Armed Services Committee, had helped me obtain my discharge. While in the Capitol, we received an invitation for a personally conducted tour of the building from Congressman "Tic" Forrester, who represented Georgia's Third District, in which Plains was located.

Along with Senator Theodore Bilbo of Mississippi, "Tic" was known as one of the most racist members of the U.S. Congress. It was obvious on our Capitol tour that he was an expert on the history of the building, but we were embarrassed by his almost constant diatribe against Catholics, Jews, and Negroes. At one time he told us that, despite his best efforts, the U.S. government was building a public-housing project in his hometown of Leesburg, and that it was almost "under the noses" of the respectable white people who lived there. We soon took our leave, without revealing that we had been accepted as residents of a similar housing project in Plains, in the heart of the "white folks'" section of town.

Back home, we moved into a small apartment in the concrete-block project with our few belongings, mostly furniture that I had built myself. Based on our net worth and very uncertain projected earnings, we were charged the minimum rent of thirty-one dollars a month. During the next sixteen months, we had a total income of less than three hundred dollars, but the following year, in 1955, our family's farm-supply business began to improve and we were able to rent a house. Our disappointing financial condition was more than overshadowed by being immersed in the close companionship of our two families, headed by my mother, Lillian, and Rosalynn's mother, Allie.

It was now time for Rosalynn and me, as parents, to assess how to accommodate the changes that had occurred since we had left Plains more than a decade ago. Our boys didn't have any grandfathers, only an aged great-grandfather. Both the grand-mothers were strong-willed and expected their own extended families to respect their matriarchal sta-tus. Also, I was no longer living in Archery, sur-rounded by black neighbors. Our Christmases had changed also with the growth of our family, with an inexorable move away from concern about our own gifts and toward the more satisfying pleasure of attempting to please our children.

Although there had not been any First Amend-ment lawsuits that forced a change, the schools were playing a greatly reduced role in students' reli-gious education and training, concentrating more on Santa Claus than on Jesus. Not having attended religious services regularly while I was in the navy, we were now full-fledged members of Plains Baptist Church, and I soon adopted the former roles of my father as a deacon and Sunday-school teacher. Our Christian faith had become more meaningful for Rosalynn and me than during the years in the navy, and we tried to impart these beliefs to our children, at home and in church.

That year, we initiated a Christmas routine that was to prevail without interruption for more than a quarter of a century. Urged by our boys, we would get up before daybreak on Christmas morning, exclaim over what Santa Claus had left (with no chimney in the housing project, we had to crack the front door to let him enter), exchange our personal gifts, and then go to my mother's house to meet my sisters and their families for another exchange of gifts. After everyone enjoyed our customary break-fast, we proceeded to meet with all of Rosalynn's kinfolks at Mother Allie's house.

By this time it was midmorning, and we usually returned home to clean up the mess we had made unwrapping our Christmas presents, assemble mech-anical toys, and let the children enjoy all their pres-ents. We would then join Rosalynn's family again for a big Christmas dinner, with each couple taking a specified dish to make up the common feast. We would spend an hour or so gossiping and enjoying each other's relaxed company, and then go back home. We usually went our separate ways during the afternoon, the men playing basketball or going hunting, the children visiting their friends, and the women relishing a few hours of solitude before we all reassembled at suppertime and a meal of leftovers brought home from dinner.

*

Over the years, I had become quite active in community affairs. I was the state leader in our primary business of producing high-quality seed peanuts, and was district governor of the Lions Clubs in our region. I also served as a Boy Scoutmaster, on the hospital authority, and as chairman of the county school board. Despite all this, I never had any ambition to seek elective office. But in 1962, the federal courts brought an end to a repressive electoral system known as the "county unit" system, which had permitted election results to be determined by counties and not by individual voters. Since the ruling came near the end of the campaign, it was applied only to the Georgia Senate during this year, in a quickly called election. I had become intensely interested in public education, which was threatened by the racial-integration issue, and fifteen days before the election, I decided that I wanted to be a state senator.

My opponent was a good and honest man, but he was supported in one of the seven counties by a political boss who was known for stuffing ballot boxes with impunity. When the votes were counted on election night, I led by 75 votes outside of Quitman County, but lost there by 224 votes. On the list of people who were claimed to have come to the courthouse to vote, 126 people had appeared alphabetically, a number of them dead or in prison.

The vote count was obviously fraudulent, but neither the Georgia Democratic Party, local judges, nor county voting officials were inclined to listen to a first-time candidate who just seemed to be a sore loser. Eventually I prevailed, primarily thanks to a courageous reporter from the *Atlanta Journal* who gave continuing front-page coverage to the shenanigans. (This election is described in my book *Turning Point*.)

I served two terms as a state senator and was later elected governor, but Rosalynn and I never let these political responsibilities interfere with our coming home to Plains for Christmas. As my other duties became more important and time-consuming, it seemed that this annual Christmas interlude became almost sacred for us. It was the one time when we could immerse ourselves for a few days among our relatives, the friends and customs of our childhood, other members of our home church, and in the fields and woods within which I had spent my early years.

Our move to Atlanta in 1971 was the biggest transformation we ever made, from a modest home in Plains to the Governor's Mansion. The magnificent structure, on an eighteen-acre lot and surrounded by ancient oak trees, really lives up to its name. I was the first governor elected after the mansion was completed, and we thoroughly enjoyed our four years there. We were thankful that I had not prevailed when, as a senator on the Appropriations Committee, I voted against funding a new governor's home. In 1960, even before this vote, when some private funds were donated, a blue-ribbon commission had gone around the nation and had skimmed off the finest furnishings of our nation's Federalist period.

It seemed that everyone in the state wanted to see the new mansion, and we kept the ground floor open every day for streams of visitors. We were grateful that garden clubs throughout Georgia competed to see which one could provide decorations during the Christmas season, which were centered on a tree always furnished by Rich's Department Store. Each day there would be different choral groups under the encircling colonnades or on the lawn to serenade the arriving and departing guests with carols.

We always went home to Plains a few days before Christmas, and one of our first tasks was to go into our own woods and find an appropriate tree. Although we had three grown sons in our family, our daughter, Amy, was the center of attention and in charge of decorations. Three years old when I became governor, she relished both the festive days in the mansion and those at home.

★

At earlier times during the holiday season, we had always feasted on the bountiful harvests from our yards and fields. In my parents' generation and even during my early married years, it was assumed that the men would sit around and discuss local and national events while the women prepared and served the food. It always seemed to us—or at least we assumed—that the wives' work in serving the family was a source of pride and gratification for them, and that their assembling in the kitchen and dining room was a natural opportunity for enjoying each other's company. When the meal was finally ready, all the husbands would crowd around the main table to eat, letting the children be served in another room; the women would eat later.

One of the most unforgettable events of our family's life was during the week before Christmas in 1974, after our oldest son was married. We were gorging ourselves with a bountiful breakfast at my mother's house when his wife walked through the dining room. He called out, "Honey, get me some more grits!" She calmly replied, "Get them yourself," and disappeared through the doorway. This sent a shock wave through everyone around the table, and has been the subject of lighthearted jokes among the men for years. I'm not sure whether this exchange had as much effect on the women, but it was clear that the young generation had introduced the first stage of new rules to the Carter family, with more equal status among husbands and wives, even during meals.

# 11

# Christmas as the First Family

★

When we moved into the White House in January 1977, we were informed that when Jackie Kennedy decided to redecorate the president's home with decor of the Federalist period she found that her buyers often had to take second choice. The Georgia Arts Commission had already acquired the finest items for our Governor's Mansion, so we felt quite at home amid the same kinds of furnishings.

I kept a personal diary during my term as president, describing on a small tape recorder the events that I knew would not be on the public record. When we returned home to Plains for good and I examined the notes for the first time, I was surprised to find that there were six thousand diary pages! It has been interesting to look back at the ones covering the four Christmas seasons, and to remember how intertwined were the personal and official experiences—how the joys and pleasures were mixed with the disappointments and tribulations.

# 1977

Although we had been there almost a year, this was our first Christmas in the White House, and we were surprised to realize how many responsibilities there were—and often pleasures—for a First Family to share the holiday season with many other people in Washington, before we could go to be with our family in Plains. As we prepared for eleven days of entertaining several thousand visitors, Rosalynn decided to cover our twenty-foot noble-fir Christmas tree in the Blue Room with twenty-five hundred ornaments made by mentally ill people, intended to show off their talents. This was an idea she had first implemented in the Governor's Mansion. The area was open to the public, and each day thousands of visitors poured through to view the tree and decorations.

There was another significant decision that we had to make: how to commemorate the season so as to include Jews, Muslims, Hindus, and even atheists. Rosalynn decided and I announced that, for four years, our Christmas cards would be a series of historic pictures of the President's House.

In order to thank all the people who had helped us during the campaign and to include our other friends and dignitaries, we came up with a list of sixty thousand people! We couldn't afford to mail this many cards ourselves and didn't want to impose on the American taxpayers, so we induced the National Democratic Party to pay the bill. In addition, we ordered several hundred large prints, and Rosalynn and I signed a few of them for special people.

We hurried home after all the festivities were over in Washington, ready to immerse ourselves as deeply as possible back in the Plains environment. As soon as we got home, we unpacked in the middle of the floor, since all the closets were full of clothes and other possessions from our previous lives. I put on my blue jeans and went out to walk in the familiar fields and woods until sundown, telling the Secret Service agents to stay as far away from me as possible. On this walk I spotted a nice Christmas tree, but I waited until the children could join me in bringing it home.

Before I became president, Rosalynn and I had disposed of all our financial holdings and placed our farms and agricultural-supply business in a blind trust, with strict orders that I was not to be informed about any of its operations or interests. But even with this complete separation, I was still eager to visit the place where, for almost a quarter of a century, we had worked to support our family.

Early the first morning at home, I went downtown to visit Carter's Warehouse, and was pleased to find that everything was in good order in the office, and that the peanut-shelling plant was operating smoothly. By the time I finished this visit, the news reporters and television crews were alerted, and they followed me as I spent a couple of hours just wandering down the main street, stopping at all the stores and shops to visit old friends. Most of them enjoyed the prospect of being on the evening news, but we usually talked long enough to forget about the surrounding observers. I was relieved that I was still just "Jimmy" to all the citizens, or "Brother Jimmy" to the men who had, at one time or another, been fellow members or deacons in our church. Always, after I became well known as governor and president, the little black children called out, "Hey, Jimmy Carter." To tourists, of course, I was "Mr. President."

The next day I decided to go quail-hunting with Rosalynn's cousin Nub Chappell, who was keeping my bird dogs while we were in Washington. During the morning, with the Secret Service agents and White House physician Bill Lukash staying in a jeep just barely in sight, we had a hard time correlating my erratic shooting with the activities of my two pointers, Bob and Lady, but at least we enjoyed a long and strenuous walk in some of the fields and woodlands that I knew so well. During the afternoon we got our act together, and found seven coveys of birds; that evening we enjoyed a nice quail supper.

Things in Plains were not as quiet and pleasant as they used to be. The town's life had been seriously disturbed when I became a presidential candidate the previous year, with a massive influx of tourists and the vendors who moved in to meet the demand for all kinds of souvenirs. It was nice this Christmas to see that eight of the fly-by-night junk shops had closed, letting old-time Plains citizens have an opportunity to regain partial control of the town. But the community had changed in another way, now that I was in office but not secluded in the White House or Camp David. The town was filled with demonstrators and people seeking recognition or special favors.

I managed to avoid a number of the special-interest groups who had descended on us, but I spent a lot of time that Christmas Eve meeting with a big delegation of distressed Georgia farmers, who had formed caravans of their largest tractors and driven long distances to assemble in Plains. I had dreaded the confrontation, but I found these would-be militants to be somewhat nervous and at the same time respectful, seeing me as a fellow farmer who would at least let them present their case to the dozens of assembled news reporters. Farm families had been doubly afflicted that year, with a terrible drought and skyrocketing fuel and fertilizer prices. For instance, a standard fertilizer formula of 5-10-15 (nitrogen-phosphate-potash) that I had sold as a warehouseman for $40 a ton before becoming governor was now $130, while the price of corn, wheat, soybeans, and cotton had not increased at all.

On Christmas Day, we turned away from any official duties and expected to have some private time with our extended family, but were dismayed when the television crews refused to stay at a distance despite our pleas. The little town was completely open, of course, and, despite the best efforts of the Secret Service agents, the cameras seemed always in our faces, practically surrounding whichever house we were visiting and attempting to film our every move.

Amy had an even worse problem—with the Secret Service agents. We looked on them as helping to give us some privacy but, as a nine-year-old, Amy saw them as just the opposite—always encroaching on hers. One morning she and her cousin Mandy noticed that the agent assigned to Amy was in the restroom, so the two girls dashed out of the house, mounted their bicycles, rode down the road a couple of hundred yards, hid the bikes behind some plum bushes, and crawled into a large corrugated pipe on a construction site. They began discussing how this could be a good hideout during the holidays, and making plans for a secret playhouse for their dolls, tea sets, and other playthings. When they finally decided to retrieve their bicycles, they stepped out of their hiding place and found a stalwart agent near each end. One of them asked, with a smile, "Are you girls ready to go home?"

In different ways, all of us were looking for time alone, or just with our friends. In my diary I wrote that in the afternoon we asked the agents to block a farm road so Rosalynn and I could slip away from everyone else to visit one of our favorite fields, an ancient Indian village site. We found nine unbroken arrowheads, exposed by heavy winter rains. She found six of them.

Somewhat reluctantly, we returned to Washington the day after Christmas.

# 1978

The national Christmas tree had fulfilled its role for many years, growing permanently in the Ellipse between the White House and the Washington Monument. This tree had been damaged by strong winds in 1977, and the following spring a storm tore it up by its roots, so we decided to plant a new tree. The National Park Service found a grown one in Pennsylvania that they could purchase and transplant, and it has now served its purpose for almost a quarter of a century.

For our Christmas card this year, Rosalynn chose a hand-colored wood engraving of the North Portico of the White House, with a stream of mounted horsemen and carriages arriving for the holiday festivities. The engraving was exactly one hundred years old, so Rosalynn decorated the White House tree with twenty-five hundred antique toys of the same era. By this time our mailing list had been corrected and brought up-to-date, but we learned to our dismay that it now contained a hundred thousand names. Once again, in addition to the cards we sent out a few large prints, signed by both of us, to special friends. Almost a thousand volunteers helped with the packaging and mailing.

Our second year in the White House had been a very good one, but the holiday season was one of the worst times of my personal life. I had been running about forty miles a week, seven miles each afternoon when I was free for an hour or so, and even farther on the weekends. I was in good physical condition, and Dr. Lukash had to convince the news reporters that my extremely low pulse rate was normal.

Our diplomatic efforts had been full and productive, with the successful Camp David Accords between Israel and Egypt, the ratification of the Panama Canal treaties by a two-thirds vote in the U.S. Senate, and the announcement on December 15 that I had negotiated a successful agreement with China's Premier Deng Xiaoping to normalize diplomatic relations with the People's Republic of China. Within our administration, we had finally resolved all the major arguments about the next year's budget, reached a consensus on how we would conclude the SALT II nuclear-arms treaty with the Soviet Union, and decided how to present our proposals to President Brezhnev and his military leaders.

We were blessed with the birth of our first granddaughter, Sarah Rosemary, during the middle of December.

It would seem that we had every reason to approach Christmas with thanksgiving, but I had a serious problem.

It was both painful and extremely embarrassing, and this is the only time I have ever made any public comment about it. I had first been afflicted when I was a young submarine officer, but this time it was much worse than ever before, and I was almost completely incapacitated from participating in any kind of public events. My initial warning was when I had to leave a Christmas party for the White House staff and press corps to receive emergency treatment and, for the first and only time during my service as president, I canceled all my scheduled events the next day and asked Vice President Walter Mondale to substitute for me. The White House physician gave me an injection of Demerol, and I slept through the annual Diplomatic Children's Reception, with Walter Cronkite and Barbara Walters trying to make excuses to the children for my absence. In fact, our young guests didn't seem to mind my failure to attend, because Amy was there to represent the First Family.

My hope was that getting back home to Plains would somehow ease my pain and discomfort, and we boarded Air Force One, accompanied by Dr. Lukash, and took off for Atlanta, where we stopped briefly to admire our beautiful little red-haired grand-daughter. Then we took a helicopter on to Plains, so far successful in concealing my problem from the public.

This year the little town was even more overrun by demonstrators, competing for the television cameras and news media that follow a president. There was a large delegation of Taiwanese protesting my recent announcement that we were normalizing diplomatic relations with mainland China, the American Farm Movement tractors had returned to the town's main street, and in the nearby fields the farmers were contending for space and attention with an assembly of Ku Klux Klansmen protesting some of my human-rights policies.

I didn't feel like confronting any of them, and I was also busy on the telephone. My diary says that I was making some final decisions about our next year's budget, encouraging the Soviets to prepare for talks on reducing nuclear arsenals, and attempting to convince the shah of Iran that he should be generous in reaching out to his people while curbing SAVAK, his brutal security police. A more pleasant duty was to call both President Anwar Sadat and Prime Minister Menachem Begin to exchange holiday greetings and to discuss how we could build on the Camp David Accords and move toward a permanent peace treaty between their two nations.

On Christmas Eve, it was still difficult for me to walk, and I had to let our son Chip and Amy go into the woods to find a tree, which we all joined in decorating. Early next morning, after the usual exchange of gifts, I went into my study and turned on the radio to see if there was any international news that might relate to our nation's projects. The top item from overseas was that President Sadat had announced to the world that his good friend Jimmy had hemorrhoids and made a public appeal for all Egyptians—Muslims and Christians—to pray on this holy day that I would be cured, because I was "a good man searching for peace."

The day after Christmas, for the first time in weeks, all the pain and discomfort went away. I was tempted to make a public announcement thanking people of all faiths for their prayers, but decided that we'd had enough publicity about my ailment. In any case, I've never received a better Christmas gift or felt more grateful for personal benefits that resulted from a nation at prayer.

# 1979

As Christmas approached in 1979, both our nation and I were obsessed with the plight of American hostages who had been captured when Iranian militants took over our embassy in Teheran during the first week in November. It seemed especially sad that such an act of international terrorism would be continuing during this holy season of peace and goodwill.

I had warned the Iranian leaders through every possible avenue that we would close all shipping and air traffic to and from Iran if any hostage were harmed, and we would launch a military attack if one of our people were killed. At the same time, I made every effort, without success, to discuss with the Iranians how we might obtain the captives.

There was not only an outpouring of concern about our hostages, but also many sincere offers of assistance. I appreciated especially the ones that were most idealistic, if naïve. One of these came from Bob Hope, who called to tell me that he was planning a trip to Iran so he could entertain the American captives on Christmas Day. He just wanted to inform me of his intentions and let me know that I need not become involved in any arrangements. I knew that his plans were hopeless. Like most other people, he underestimated the deep hatred toward America and the militant attitude of the Ayatollah Khomeini and those who were holding the prisoners. All mediation efforts had been rebuffed, even including those of Muslim convert Muhammad Ali.

Although we had decided to restrict our personal travels, Rosalynn and I felt that we should have the regular holiday observances at the White House. We realized how much pleasure our visitors got from such social affairs, and we didn't want to let the Iranian terrorists have the satisfaction of interfering in these precious events. For many afternoons and nights during the holiday season, we followed the tradition of America's First Families by holding a constant series of receptions.

Among many others, we entertained members of the Secret Service and the executive police around the White House, with all their families—about a thousand people. We had the directors of the intelligence community, Office of Management and Budget, General Services Administration, Federal Emergency Management Agency, Cabinet members, our own staff members, and the White House press corps. It seemed that there was a never-ending list of other organizations and agencies, and we scheduled as many as possible to come to visit us in the President's House.

Even during the parties, I still had to deal with sensitive issues involving Iran. One of them was what to do with the deposed shah, who was now living in exile after revolutionaries overthrew his government. Having become Iran's leader in 1941, he had kept his country closely allied with the United States during and since World War II, and we felt obligated to help find him a place to stay. The shah was a proud and demanding leader concerning accommodations for himself and his family, and the revolutionary government was exerting political pressure and threats against any nation willing to accept him. He had been to Egypt, the Bahamas, and Mexico, but either they had asked him to leave or he found living conditions unsatisfactory. Now terminally ill with cancer, the shah was in Texas for treatment, but he was insisting on going to some small and neutral nation.

I remember that, during a reception for about twelve hundred members of Congress and their family members, I was beckoned from the receiving line to take a call from Panamanian president Omar Torrijos, who informed me that he was extending an invitation to the shah to leave San Antonio and come to Panama, where he could continue medical treatment. After the shah's doctors reported that he was able to travel and that the stay in a private home on Contadora Island would be beneficial, I called him. He said he was very pleased with the arrangements, especially because he had been "ripped off" in the Bahamas and Mexico. He was grateful that he would be accepting an invitation to Panama as an honored guest, and not as an exile going into sanctuary.

One of the most emotional events that Christmas season came when we had the annual lighting of the national tree on the Ellipse. Amy and I planned a big surprise for the ceremony. When the television cameras focused on her at the crucial moment, she threw the switch but no lights lit up on the tree except the single Star of Hope on top—a symbolic acknowledgment that we were not celebrating while our hostages were being held, but were confident that all of them would return safely and to freedom. We had placed a row of small trees around the park, one for each hostage, with blue lights on them. Afterward, I received more favorable comments about the surprise lighting than about almost anything else I've ever done. I had thought this was the first event of its kind, but someone told me that the national tree was not lighted for three years during World War II.

In addition to being in charge of all the normal White House events, Rosalynn was busy promoting the welfare of refugees from Vietnam and Cambodia—human flotsam from the Vietnam War. There were tens of thousands of them in crowded camps just across the border in Thailand, permanently displaced from their homes and now huddled together and largely forgotten. I had decided to accept fourteen thousand per month as immigrants to our country, and was attempting to persuade other

nations to welcome them or contribute funds through the United Nations high commissioner for refugees.

Rosalynn decided to publicize their plight with a personal visit to their camps during the Christmas season. After returning home and during the holidays, she went to the United Nations, spoke to the Council on Foreign Relations and other influential groups, and was interviewed on a number of television talk shows. She appealed for financial contributions, and there was an outpouring of gifts from Americans who still felt responsible for meeting this last challenge from the war. Perhaps some Christian donors remembered the plight of a family when there was no room at the inn in Bethlehem.

In addition to all the public events, our kinfolks, old acquaintances from Georgia, and our children's friends were pouring in to visit us, and the White House was full of people every time I went home to our private living quarters. This was always an enticement for me to work longer hours in the Oval Office. One thing that helped was that I was still running several miles late every afternoon, either on a winding trail on the South Lawn or alongside the C & O Canal.

Rosalynn and I were looking forward to getting out of Washington, and we began to discuss whether we should go home to Plains. For twenty-six uninterrupted years, since the year my daddy died, we had been with our extended families for Christmas, and this year we especially needed a few days of comfort and companionship among relatives and close friends. It was a grievous disappointment, but we finally decided that it was best to stay where I would have a large supportive staff nearby, and a superb worldwide communications system—just in case there were any fast-breaking developments involving the hostages. We decided instead to go to Camp David.

This Christmas season I had another problem: a serious political challenge from Senator Ted Kennedy, who had announced two months earlier that he would replace me as the Democratic nominee for president. Polls during November had shown that he was ahead by a margin of three to one, and we hoped that this was just a transient negative reaction to the kidnapping of our hostages. By mid-December, I was gaining ground, and just before leaving Washington for a few days at Camp David, I talked to one of my senior advisers, Clark Clifford, about the possibility of persuading Kennedy to withdraw from the race.

Clifford responded that this was a hopeless request and that, in any case, it was good for me to have an opponent, just to keep me and my supporters on our toes. He drew a rough parallel with a story about fishermen in Iceland who caught turbot, one of the most delicious of all fish, whose flesh was especially firm because of their constant rapid swimming. The captured turbot were kept alive on the way to American and European markets, but in large tanks they tended to become fat and sluggish. The Icelanders solved the problem by putting one small barracuda in each tank. They would sacrifice three or four turbot for barracuda meals during the voyage, but the other thousands stayed lean and tasty. Personally, I preferred not to have any "barracudas" in the Democratic Party ranks, and especially at Christmastime.

Although we were wishing for a restful holiday at Camp David, I realized when I unpacked my briefcase that the campaign staff had given me a list of several hundred telephone calls to make to key Democrats to respond to Kennedy's challenge. Rosalynn helped me, and we began by concentrating our calls in Iowa. The response was good, with many of the people telling us that early support for my opponent was dissipating. I was becoming fairly confident that I was even and pulling ahead, which helped boost our lagging Christmas spirit.

To get away from the telephone for a few hours, I walked down the mountain and went fly-fishing in Hunting Creek. I didn't catch anything, but enjoyed the fresh air and solitude. On the way back to our cabin, I realized that it was going to be a lonely Christmas. Our last-minute decision to stay at Camp David had caught our sons and their families by surprise, and they were spending the holidays in Plains or with in-laws, so Rosalynn, Amy, and I were to be the only family members there.

More than any others in our family, Amy was immersed in the lives of the White House staff, spending hours in the kitchen and other places with the cooks, stewards, laundry workers, ushers, maids, butlers, and maintenance men. When I mentioned how empty Camp David seemed, she replied that very few of these loyal workers had ever been to Camp David, although many of them had served in the White House for several decades and some were approaching retirement. We agreed with her suggestion to invite all of them to come up and spend Christmas Day with us, with no responsibilities at all except that the Filipino stewards already on duty would prepare a festive meal for everybody.

We three exchanged personal gifts in our cabin quite early Christmas morning, read the Christmas story once again, and then, at daylight, we began calling our families in Plains and talked to everyone we could get on the phone. Afterward, we spent several hours with two busloads of our friends from the White House, who brought their families with them. We enjoyed acting as guides, showing off the various cabins, the swimming pool, the bowling alley, the room where we had Sunday religious services, and answering their questions about how the Egyptians and Israelis had lived and worked during the long peace talks. After a Christmas dinner of turkey with all the trimmings and individual photographs with each family, we waved goodbye to the buses. Their visit had turned our potentially lonely Christmas Day into one that we would never forget.

At the same time, I couldn't forget about the American hostages being held in Teheran, and was wondering what else I might do to hasten their release. The next morning, I began calling key

members of the United Nations Security Council and other world leaders, urging them to support our proposal for financial sanctions against Iran as long as they were holding our people.

I maintained my hopes that we would soon be getting better news from the region, but the day after Christmas I was informed that the Soviets were moving planeloads of troops into Afghanistan. We monitored 215 flights, which meant a couple of regiments were in the invading force, with maybe a total of ten thousand men. After once again calling the leaders of key nations around the world, this time to urge them to stand with us in condemning the Soviet invasion, I returned to Washington to decide what to do about this additional threat. It was related at least indirectly to the problem we were already facing in Iran. We surmised that President Brezhnev was taking advantage of trouble in the region to consolidate Russia's hold on Afghanistan and would then move through either Iran or Pakistan to realize his nation's ancient desire for access to a warm-water port.

A few days after I returned to Washington, a new national poll showed me surging ahead of Kennedy, 58 to 38 percent. It seemed that threatening news from the Middle East region helped to increase my public support. Although there were no encouraging signals from Iran, we tried to maintain the nation's hope that, within the next few weeks, our hostages would be returning home.

# 1980

Twelve months later, in 1980, we approached Christmas with few reasons for celebration. I had lost the election and would soon be out of office. Fifty-two hostages were still being held in Iran, but we were encouraged by reports from the Algerians that the Ayatollah Khomeini was contemplating their release during the holiday season. We were maintaining maximum economic and political sanctions from as wide a range of nations as we could recruit to join us, and these pressures on the Iranian leaders were increasing. After almost fourteen months, it was becoming obvious in Teheran that their continuing act of international terrorism was counterproductive.

An additional crisis had arisen for them when Iraq invaded Iran in September 1980. However, we would not respond to blackmail or pay ransom, and I rejected their demand that we apologize publicly and also provide a $25 billion fund to be held in escrow to settle any of their claims against the United States. Instead, we had tied up half this amount of Iranian assets in American and foreign banks, which I had already decided to continue holding as claims against them. This was the basis for the hostages' subsequent release, which we would finally negotiate during the last few hours that I was in office.

Now, seven weeks after the November election, I had been able to put its results behind me, because I still had all my regular duties to perform, and partially because I had to think up all kinds of positive factors to ease Rosalynn's disappointment and anger about our loss. After a surprisingly productive "lame duck" session with the Congress, we decided to go to Plains for a brief visit, although I continued to concentrate on my highest priority of freeing the hostages. We were finally negotiating through the Algerians, who we hoped would be permitted to visit all of our people and give me a report on their condition. Still, we didn't let our hopes rise too high, because they had been dashed so many times during the past year.

All our children and grandchildren had come to Washington before Christmas to be with us for some of the White House festivities, and also to help us begin packing to go home. Rosalynn decided that the decorations should be as old-fashioned and nostalgic as possible, and our tree was decorated with hundreds of nineteenth-century dolls, all with porcelain heads. Our Christmas cards had become a fine way to express our friendship and thanks to a large group of people who had become friends or at least political acquaintances, and Rosalynn had stayed on the lookout all year for the best old painting of the White House. She had finally chosen a remarkable water scene showing the President's House in the distance when Andrew Jackson was living there, with a small sailboat and a rowboat in the foreground. (The stream is now in a culvert beneath Constitution Avenue, part of Washington's sewer system.) This time, we sent out 120,000 cards, with a number of enlarged prints, as before. By now, they had become collectors' items, especially the relatively small number that included our personal signatures.

In planning for the national tree, I invited the families of the hostages to meet with us. After giving them a secret briefing on all I was doing to bring their loved ones home, I asked what they wanted to do about the Christmas lights. They all asked us to leave the tree as it had been the previous year, dark and green, with just the Star of Hope shining at the top. Later, I agreed to a request from the National Association of Broadcasters to light the tree for 417 seconds, one for each day the hostages had been in captivity.

We planned an extraordinary series of parties this year, much more personal in nature, designed to thank all the people who had helped us during our time in Washington. I was feeling especially grateful to the members of Congress, who had given me a good batting average on my legislative proposals during the past four years and had been especially helpful following my defeat in November. We had passed some very important and controversial bills, including a historic decision on an issue that had been debated since Alaska became a state, while President Dwight Eisenhower was in office. This act more than doubled the size of our national-park system and tripled the wilderness areas. At the same time, we authorized drilling for 95 percent of Alaska's potential oil reserves, while protecting the small but precious wildlife refuge adjoining the Beaufort Sea. In addition, we completed four years of work on laws that required strict energy savings on automobiles, machinery, homes, and appliances, and deregulated prices to discourage waste of oil and natural gas and, at the same time, to increase domestic production.

We expanded our invitation list for the season's parties to include families of those who had worked directly in my administration, and our children and even small grandchildren joined in as hosts. Our staff surprised us by bringing in snowmaking machines and covering the South Lawn two feet deep with white powder. We first took the children out and rode on toboggans and cross-country skis, and then invited the White House staff to join us. The kids had a snowman contest, and the next night we had an ice show, the cast led by Olympic figure-skating champion Peggy Fleming.

I learned that the Cabinet officers and White House staff had taken up a collection to buy me a going-away gift, and that it was to be a Jeep. As a better alternative, I hinted that I'd like to resume a former hobby of making furniture. This resulted in my most enjoyable and long-lasting of all Christmas gifts. The money that had already been collected was given to Sears, Roebuck, with instructions to provide every tool and piece of equipment that I would need. Our garage in Plains would become my woodworking shop, and since then I have supplied the needs in our own home, furnished an entire mountain cabin, built baby cradles to encourage the production of additional grandchildren, and made a few chairs, tables, desks, cabinets, and other items to be auctioned for the benefit of The Carter Center.* Walking the twenty steps from my computer and immersing myself in the woodshop is a perfect way to refresh my mind and bring an end to writer's block when I'm working on a book or a poem.

When we got home two days before Christmas, Mama was recovering from a broken hip and trying to be cheerful while demonstrating small steps with a walker. Amy went with me into the woods, and

---

* The Carter Center is a nongovernmental organization established by Rosalynn and me in 1982 to promote peace, human rights, and democracy, and to alleviate human suffering. We now have active programs in sixty-five of the poorest nations.

we finally found a small but acceptable tree that we could decorate. We also found a nice arrowhead on the way.

Rosalynn and I spent a lot of time in our house this Christmas trying to decide what we would have to change when we came back to Plains. It had been ten years since we lived there, and we hadn't spent full time in our home in fourteen years, since I began running for governor in 1966. The yards were all washed away, the house was really in need of cleaning and repair, and it seemed to have shrunk considerably. We would have to fill up the garage with crates and boxes just to unload the moving van, and put a floor in the attic for permanent storage. The main problem was how we would ever find space for the hundreds of books that we absolutely had to keep. Bookshelves would have to be the first products of the woodworking tools.

Since we had planted pine, maple, and other trees around the White House from our Georgia farm, I asked for cuttings and seedlings to carry home with us to Plains. We planted Andrew Jackson magnolias, Harry Truman boxwoods, and also lindens, hemlock, goldenrain trees, and an American elm in our yard. Rosalynn had replaced a dying

Japanese maple that Mrs. Grover Cleveland had planted on the South Lawn in 1893, and we brought a cutting from the new one. Later, we added a George Washington poplar from Mount Vernon.

As always, we walked down the street in Plains, being welcomed and quietly consoled by friends with whom we would soon be living once again. This time, there were not so many television cameras. We presumed that they were following Ronald Reagan out in California. During the heyday of enormous tourism in the town, *Penthouse* publisher Larry Flynt had bought the *Plains Monitor* newspaper, and when we stopped by to visit the local editor, he showed us a bicycle for two he had won in a raffle. He loaned it to us, and we rode it back home and then a few miles out to the Pond House, where Mama was living. The gears hung up, and we left it there. The next day, our children surprised us with a pair of bicycles for our Christmas present. I gave Rosalynn a small television set for the bedroom, and she gave me a book on woodworking and some fly-tying equipment.

One of the biggest challenges of this Christmas season had tested my waning influence as a lame-duck president. Trivial Pursuit had become wildly popular, but there was a genuine shortage of the game, and, predictably, this was what all the children in our family described as "the main thing I want!" Normal shopping excursions around Washington by our personal staff had been fruitless, so we asked them to escalate their efforts. Finally, the day before we were to leave for Plains, one of our domestic advisers reported that he had been able to obtain two of the games from the manufacturer. (He denied that he was giving us his own.)

On Christmas morning, our family was gathered around the game, and we were excited by one of the questions: "Who was the first American president born in a hospital?," with the answer being "Jimmy Carter." We were not so thrilled when we joined probably thousands of other groups throughout America in exclaiming over the answer to another question: "Who said, 'Sometimes when I look at my children, I wish I had remained a virgin'?" The answer was "The president's mother, Lillian Carter."

I proposed a question of my own that few people were able to answer: "Which former presidents, if any, are *not* buried within the continental limits of the United States?" Richard Nixon and Gerald Ford were not buried, and I was soon to become the third. It was good to remember that all former presidents had not passed away.

During Christmas afternoon, we drove out into the country about ten miles to examine the rural school that would be Amy's when we came back home, and that night the assembled White House news reporters threw a farewell party under the town water tank for the people of Plains. The next day, we returned to Camp David.

When we arrived, we found that there were about two inches of snow on the ground. We had had a lot of snow during my first two years in office, and had taken up cross-country skiing. Now, once again, we were eager to try the mountain trails. First we went out to ski around the outside of the security fence, and then I came back inside to join our son Jack on the rocky nature trail behind our cabin. While I was going down a steep hill, my right ski hit a rock, and I fell and broke my left collarbone. We went to Bethesda Naval Hospital to have it X-rayed, set, and strapped, and I returned to Camp David.

My arm was throbbing with pain, but I asked Secretary of State Ed Muskie to bring an Algerian delegation to meet with me. They were the only intermediaries with whom the Ayatollah Khomeini would communicate, and had just been permitted to visit with the hostages. They reported that all the prisoners were in good shape, and forty-two of the fifty-two had sent letters to their folks back home. The Iranians had not interfered with these visits. That afternoon, we formulated our final proposal for the Algerians to deliver to the Iranians for the release of the hostages. It was fairly harsh, retaining enough Iranian gold and bank deposits to cover all American claims against Iran, any disputes to be resolved by the rulings of an international court. I also worked on my farewell speech that evening.

Our usual practice was to invite the army chaplain to come from a nearby military base to Camp David to conduct services every week, and we were looking forward to a special Christmas ceremony. But this Sunday morning, the roads were iced over and the fog was too thick for the army chaplain to travel, so we and some of the navy men on duty took turns reading Luke's account of the birth of Jesus, and then we had a discussion of the subsequent flight of the family into Egypt.

The next day, we collected our fly rods, skis, and the outdoor clothing that we kept on the mountain, to be crated and shipped to Plains. It was sad to say a final goodbye to Camp David, but a happy time to know that the Americans in Iran were safe, and to have renewed hope that our efforts to secure their release were now quite promising. In fact, my prayers for every hostage to return home safe and to freedom would soon be answered.

By New Year's Eve, we were back in Washington and went to a party with top staff members—without any regrets to see the end of 1980. I had no idea what the coming year would bring for my family and me, but all of us were reconciled to leaving the White House and looking to the future. A few days later, I stood for several hours in the Oval Office and I shook hands, had a photograph taken, and personally thanked almost fourteen hundred people who had worked with us in the White House and the Executive Office Building next door. I could feel the bones rubbing together in my strapped left shoulder every time someone shook my right hand, but the pain didn't detract from the pride that we shared as our team members mentioned their own roles in promoting peace, environmental quality, and human rights in America and around the world.

My last hours in office were filled with high drama. I never went to bed Sunday or Monday night, and we finally realized that our intense negotiations had been successful when Tuesday morning dawned—inauguration day.

The Iranians yielded on all the major points of our discussions, agreeing to our holding $12 billion to resolve financial claims, and to the safe release of all the American captives. Two hours before my term was to end, I was informed that all of them were in a plane at the end of the runway in Teheran, poised to take off for Wiesbaden, Germany, where they would be given physical examinations and where I would later meet them. The plane was in the air with all the hostages on board while my successor was making his acceptance speech. We celebrated all the way to Georgia, my last ride in Air Force One.

# 12

# Christmas During Recent Years

★

It took us only a brief time after we returned to Plains to immerse ourselves in the life of the community. We stayed there at home as much as possible, but kept busy. I read all my personal-diary notes, wrote a book about my experiences as president, refurbished our house, sold our warehouse business, became reacquainted with our farmland, raised money to build a presidential library in Atlanta, and founded The Carter Center—all within little more than a year.

It was now time to devote more attention to our expanding family. Our sons were all married, we had three grandchildren, and Amy was a thirteen-year-old in high school. We had been delighted with the wedding of each of our children, enjoying pleasant visions of a growing number of grandchildren gathering in Plains every Christmas for joyous reunions. Instead we confronted what we soon realized was a universal feeling of competition with new in-laws, who expected the same children to be with them each year. It was hard to admit that the other grandparents had equal rights to our grandchildren. Although we never struggled directly with our competitors, there was something of a strain among the married couples as they tried to appease both sets of parents and decide themselves where to spend Christmas Day.

Rosalynn and I are always in Plains for Christmas, and over the years our children have lived in different places: Rhode Island, California, Tennessee, Louisiana, Illinois, Ohio, Bermuda, and various locations in Georgia. After a couple of years, we decided that one of our main goals was to hold our family together as much as possible, so we just relaxed and let the different families decide whether they preferred to be with us or somewhere else. We began a custom of inviting all of them, children and grandchildren, to join us a day or two after Christmas for a vacation trip together. This time fit in quite well with the normal holiday for children in school, and we have been able to save up enough money and frequent-flyer miles to pay the bills.

The first two years we went on Caribbean cruises, and had some wonderful experiences. Aboard ship, all members of the family were free to choose our own favorite activities, but we were close together and shared the scrumptious meals, dance lessons, good movies, floor shows at night, snorkeling and exploring around the islands, and other good times. In order to defray the cost, Rosalynn and I agreed with the cruise line to give a lecture and to answer questions from the hundreds of other passengers, and I signed copies of my book on the way back to Miami on the last day at sea. The following year, Rosalynn was invited to christen and be godmother of a new cruise ship, *Sovereign of the Seas,* and our entire family was invited to share the holiday trip.

Each year since then, we have tried to let our grandchildren choose the holiday destination, which has been quite an adventure in itself. We've been to New Mexico and Colorado skiing; to Oaxaca, the Yucatán, Belize, Panama, Key West, Costa Rica; and fishing along the Gulf Coast. For the little grandchildren, Disney World has been a favorite destination.

In 1988, we decided to do something different

with our Christmas cards. By then we had six grand-children, and we asked each of them to craft an original holiday scene, without their parents' guidance. Jason, thirteen, did a surrealistic but recognizable Santa Claus; James, eleven, painted the Baby Jesus in a manger with an enormous star overhead; Sarah, ten, decided on six stockings with the kids' names on them; Joshua, four, contributed a multicolored rainbow; and Jeremy and Maggie, less than two, used finger paints to express their hopes and thanks for the season. This card turned out to be the most popular one we've ever had.

## 13

# Best Christmas of All?

★

It's not easy to choose our best Christmas, but it may have been in 1991. It involved Curtis Jackson, a black man who was born and spent his early adulthood on the farm of Rosalynn's grandfather, whom everyone called "Captain" Murray. Curtis had eight brothers and six sisters, and he remembers the wonderful days of Christmas in their family. "We knew what we was going to get, and looked forward to it every year. It would be an apple and some dry grapes."

For a number of years, Curtis was a day laborer, and then, later, graduated to having crops of his own, which he worked "on halves." Mr. Captain furnished the mules, equipment, and land, and Curtis and his wife, Martha, did all the work and got half the crop. Martha had two children, but Curtis said "she had a weak system," and both children died as infants. The family had a monthly draw of fifteen dollars, with which they would acquire store-bought groceries, tobacco and snuff, and clothing. He said this was a lot more than the thirty dollars his daddy got each month, with fifteen children to feed.

After Mr. Captain retired from farming, Curtis got a job on a sawmill crew. He would get up each morning at four o'clock, Martha would fix his noon meal in a gallon lard can, and he would walk to the center of Plains, where a logging truck picked him up to go to a large sawmill in Dumas, about five miles west of town. There the individual crews would be sent out to cut down the trees, lop off all limbs, and load the logs on the truck. During his seventh year there, Curtis's chain saw slipped when he was cutting limbs, and severed his right leg just above the knee.

When he could walk again, Curtis got a job as handyman at the local nursing home, which had formerly been the Wise Sanitarium, where my mother had been a nurse. He worked there another seven years, and then Rosalynn and I hired him to help me tend to our yard and keep a path cleared around our fishpond.

Curtis was a willing worker, always laughing about something, and a wonderful raconteur. He loved to describe farm life as he remembered it from his boyhood. Although we didn't know each other in those early days, he was a contemporary of mine, and we shared a lot of similar experiences. Curtis and I had long conversations, and he helped refresh my memory as I took notes that later surfaced in my book *An Hour Before Daylight*. He had a lot of trouble with his wooden leg, so one day we drove to a nearby city where he was fitted with a well-designed prosthesis. For the first time since his accident, he could walk without pain.

When Curtis's wife, Martha, became ill, we went to visit her, and were appalled at their ramshackle house. It had no heat except a small woodstove, we could see through the walls in several places, and there were old buckets sitting around to catch the streams of water that came through the roof when it rained. Curtis said, "It's good on clear nights. We can see the stars from our bed." Some of the sills had rotted out, and the limber floorboards bent down like a trampoline with a person's weight. In October, Martha developed what Curtis called "high blood," and had to be admitted to the nursing home.

Rosalynn and I decided that the Jacksons needed a new house, and we talked it over with the folks in our church. We were already involved with Habitat for Humanity, an organization devoted to providing decent homes for needy families. The international headquarters is in Americus, just ten miles from Plains, and Curtis and Martha easily qualified for the program.

Habitat's normal policy is that the future home-owner's family members should put in five hundred hours of work and pay the full cost of their new house, including materials and labor. At the same time, we follow the Biblical prohibition against charging interest to a poor person. With twenty years to pay, this would keep Curtis's monthly payments low enough so he could afford them from his Social Security income. Curtis couldn't read or write, so we prepared the papers, and he helped our volunteer work crews in clearing off a site alongside his old house and preparing the foundation for the new home. Since he was physically handicapped, his wife was ill, and he had no children, some of the neighbors and volunteers helped Curtis fulfill the work requirement.

The people in Plains responded enthusiastically to our call for volunteers, and we soon had enough workers to set Christmas Eve as a target date for completion of the house. We spent the last two days and nights putting on the final touches: laying carpets and tile floors, planting shrubbery, trimming the doors and windows, installing a new stove, refrigerator, and heating system, and hanging paintings on the walls. Our children and grandchildren who came to Plains for Christmas joined us, and we labored until dark on Christmas Eve to complete the multitude of small tasks that always confront builders at the last minute.

Then, after dark, Curtis picked up Martha and brought her home to sleep in their new house. I think it's true to say that most of us had forgotten all about Santa Claus. But Curtis and Martha hadn't.

*

We still have a lot to learn about all the nuances and glories of Christmas.

# About the Author

*

Jimmy Carter, who served as thirty-ninth president of the United States, was born in Plains, Georgia, in 1924. After leaving the White House, he and his wife, Rosalynn, founded the Atlanta-based Carter Center, a nonprofit organization that works to prevent and resolve conflicts, enhance freedom and democracy, and improve health around the world.